pastries and breads

Published in 2007 by Murdoch Books Pty Limited.
www.murdochbooks.com.au

Murdoch Books Australia
Pier 8/9, 23 Hickson Road
Millers Point NSW 2000
Phone: + 61 (0) 2 8220 2000
Fax: + 61 (0) 2 8220 2558

Murdoch Books UK Limited
Erico House, 6th Floor
93–99 Upper Richmond Road
Putney, London SW15 2TG
Phone: + 44 (0) 20 8785 5995
Fax: + 44 (0) 20 8785 5985

Chief Executive: Juliet Rogers
Publishing Director: Kay Scarlett

Design Manager: Vivien Valk
Concept & Art Direction: Sarah Odgers
Design: Jacqueline Duncan
Editor and Project Manager: Rhiain Hull
Production: Monique Layt
Photographer: Jared Fowler
Stylist: Cherise Koch
Food preparation: Alan Wilson
Introduction text: Leanne Kitchen
Recipes developed by the Murdoch Books Test Kitchen

National Library of Australia Cataloguing-in-Publication Data
Pastries and breads. Includes index.
ISBN 978 1 92125 908 1 (pbk.).
1. Pastry. Cookery (Bread). I. Price, Jane (Jane Paula Wynn).
(Series: Kitchen Classics; 6). 641.71

A catalogue record for this book is available from the British Library

Printed by 1010 Printing International Limited in 2007. PRINTED IN CHINA.
Reprinted 2007.

CONVERSION GUIDE: You may find cooking times vary depending on the oven you are using. For fan-forced ovens, as a general rule, set the oven temperature to 20°C (35°F) lower than indicated in the recipe. We have used 20 ml (4 teaspoon) tablespoon measures. If you are using a 15 ml (3 teaspoon) tablespoon, for most recipes the difference will not be noticeable. However, for recipes using baking powder, gelatine, bicarbonate of soda (baking soda), small amounts of flour, add an extra teaspoon for each tablespoon specified.

pastries and breads

THE BAKING RECIPES YOU MUST HAVE

SERIES EDITOR **JANE PRICE**

MURDOCH BOOKS

CONTENTS

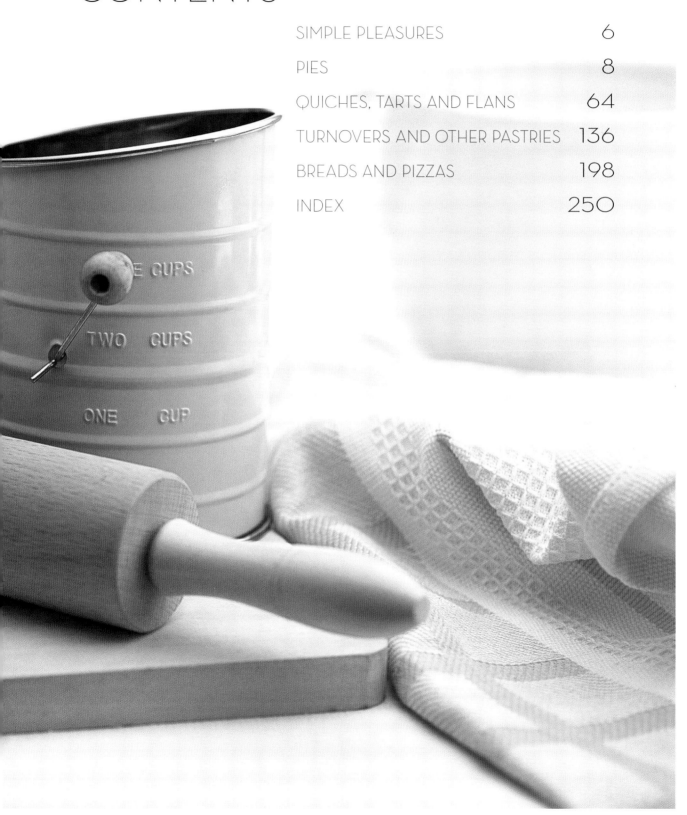

SIMPLE PLEASURES

Mmmmmmmmm ... pie. The gorgeous smell of just-baked pastry that fills the kitchen after you bake a pie is, arguably, only bettered by the aromas that rise from steamingly hot loaves of bread, just whisked from the oven. Those sweet, earthy whiffs have been ruining appetites for eons — for who on earth can resist a warm slice of homey pie or freshly made bread, even if it is nearly dinnertime? And to think that, in the early years of pie-making (we're talking twelfth-century England here), the pastry of a pie wasn't even eaten; rather it functioned as the serving vessel for what lurked inside and was, from all accounts, rock hard and pretty awful. Early versions of bread were similiarly rustic; food historians conjecture that these were no more than crude pastes of wheat, hardened over fire. What a difference some millennia make! Now, thanks to the wide availability of great ingredients, and our sophisticated home ovens, we can bake delicious pastry doughs and gooey bread doughs into whatever our hearts desire.

In *Pastries and Breads*, you'll find ideas and inspiration galore. There are hearty, chunky, main-course offerings like beef and red wine pies plus daintier, individual morsels too (empanandas, turnovers and filo parcels). Then, as pies loose their tops and morph into quiches, flans and tarts, there's more elegant fare, worthy of grand dinners or celebratory picnics. Sweet pies go completely without saying and here, fillings run the entire gamut — choose from custard, rhubarb, apple, treacle, key lime, berry or cherry, for example. Breads are an equally varied mob and, despite what you may have heard, are a cinch to make. From soda, Turkish, olive and sourdough sorts to banana, Greek Easter and even pizza, you'll be amazed at the good tastes and simple pleasures that result when you take the time to bake your own.

PIES

BEEF AND RED WINE PIES

60 ml (2 fl oz/¼ cup) oil

1.5 kg (3 lb 5 oz) chuck steak, cubed

2 onions, chopped

1 garlic clove, crushed

30 g (1 oz/¼ cup) plain (all-purpose) flour

310 ml (10¾ fl oz/1¼ cups) good-quality dry red wine

500 ml (17 fl oz/2 cups) beef stock

2 bay leaves

2 thyme sprigs

2 carrots, chopped

500 g (1 lb 2 oz) shortcrust (pie) pastry

500 g (1 lb 2 oz) block ready-made puff pastry, thawed

1 egg, lightly beaten

MAKES 6

Lightly grease six metal pie tins measuring 9 cm (3½ inches) along the base and 3 cm (1¼ inches) deep.

Heat 2 tablespoons of the oil in a large frying pan and brown the chuck steak in batches. Remove from the pan. Heat the remaining oil in the same pan, add the onion and garlic and stir over medium heat until golden brown. Add the flour and stir over medium heat for 2 minutes, or until well browned. Remove from the heat and gradually stir in the combined wine and stock.

Return to the heat and stir until the mixture boils and thickens. Return the meat to the pan, add the bay leaves and thyme and simmer for 1 hour. Add the carrot and simmer for another 45 minutes, or until the meat and carrot are tender and the sauce has thickened. Season, then remove the bay leaves and thyme. Allow to cool.

Preheat the oven to 200°C (400°F/Gas 6). Divide the shortcrust pastry into six portions and roll out each piece between two sheets of baking paper to a 25 cm (10 inch) square, 3 mm (⅛ inch) thick. Cut a circle from each shortcrust sheet big enough to line the base and side of each pie tin. Place in the tins and trim the edges. Line each pastry shell with baking paper and fill with baking beads or uncooked rice. Place on a baking tray and bake for 8 minutes. Remove the paper and beads and bake for another 8 minutes, or until the pastry is lightly browned. Allow to cool.

Divide the puff pastry into six portions and roll each piece between two sheets of baking paper to a square. Cut circles from the squares of dough, to fit the tops of the pie tins. Divide the filling evenly among the pastry cases and brush the edges with some of the beaten egg. Cover with a puff pastry round and trim any excess pastry, pressing the edges with a fork to seal. Cut a slit in the top of each pie. Brush the pie tops with the remaining beaten egg and bake for 20–25 minutes, or until the pastry is cooked and golden brown.

PREPARATION TIME: 50 MINUTES   COOKING TIME: 2 HOURS 40 MINUTES

NOTE: You can make a family-sized pie using the same ingredients, but substituting a 23 cm (9 inch) metal pie tin. Bake in a 200°C (400°F/Gas 6) oven for 30–35 minutes. Any remaining pastry can be rolled and used to decorate the pie, or frozen for later use.

MOROCCAN CHICKEN PIE

200 g (7 oz) butter
1.5 kg (3 lb 5 oz) chicken, cut into
4 portions
1 large onion, finely chopped
3 teaspoons ground cinnamon
1 teaspoon ground ginger
2 teaspoons ground cumin
$\frac{1}{4}$ teaspoon cayenne pepper
$\frac{1}{2}$ teaspoon ground turmeric
$\frac{1}{2}$ teaspoon saffron threads soaked in
2 tablespoons warm water
125 ml (4 fl oz/$\frac{1}{2}$ cup) chicken stock
4 eggs, lightly beaten
25 g (1 oz) chopped coriander (cilantro)
3 tablespoons chopped flat-leaf (Italian)
parsley
50 g ($1\frac{3}{4}$ oz/$\frac{1}{3}$ cup) chopped almonds
30 g (1 oz/$\frac{1}{4}$ cup) icing (confectioners')
sugar
375 g (13 oz) filo pastry
icing (confectioners') sugar, extra, to dust

SERVES 6–8

Preheat the oven to 180°C (350°F/Gas 4). Grease a 30 cm (12 inch) pizza tray.

Melt 40 g ($1\frac{1}{2}$ oz) of the butter in a large frying pan. Add the chicken, onion, 2 teaspoons of the cinnamon, all the other spices and the stock. Season, cover and simmer for 30 minutes, or until the chicken is cooked through.

Remove the chicken from the sauce. When cool enough to handle, remove the meat from the bones, discard the skin and bones and shred the meat into thin strips.

Bring the liquid in the pan to a simmer and add the eggs. Cook the mixture, stirring constantly, until the eggs are cooked and the mixture is quite dry. Add the chicken, chopped coriander and parsley, season well and mix. Remove from the heat.

Bake the almonds on a baking tray until golden brown. Cool slightly, then blend in a food processor or spice grinder with the icing sugar and remaining cinnamon until they resemble coarse crumbs.

Melt the remaining butter. Place a sheet of filo on the pizza tray and brush with melted butter. Place another sheet on top in a pinwheel effect and brush with butter. Continue brushing and layering until you have used eight sheets. Put the chicken mixture on top and sprinkle with the almond mixture.

Fold the overlapping filo over the top of the filling. Place a sheet of filo over the top and brush with butter. Continue to layer buttered filo over the top in the same pinwheel effect until you have used eight sheets. Tuck the overhanging edges over the pie to form a neat round parcel. Brush well with the remaining butter. Bake the pie for 40–45 minutes, or until cooked through and golden. Dust with icing sugar before serving.

PREPARATION TIME: 30 MINUTES   COOKING TIME: 1 HOUR 20 MINUTES

COUNTRY VEGETABLE PIES

PASTRY

250 g (9 oz/2 cups) plain
(all-purpose) flour
125 g (4½ oz) butter, chilled and cubed
2 egg yolks
2–3 tablespoons iced water

FILLING

2 new potatoes, cubed
350 g (12 oz) butternut pumpkin
(squash), cubed
100 g (3½ oz) broccoli, cut into
small florets
100 g (3½ oz) cauliflower, cut into
small florets
1 zucchini (courgette), grated
1 carrot, grated
3 spring onions (scallions), chopped
90 g (3¼ oz/¾ cup) grated
cheddar cheese
125 g (4½ oz/½ cup) ricotta cheese
50 g (1¾ oz/½ cup) grated
parmesan cheese
3 tablespoons chopped flat-leaf
(Italian) parsley
1 egg, lightly beaten

MAKES 6

To make the pastry, sift the flour into a bowl. Using your fingertips, rub in the butter until the mixture resembles fine breadcrumbs. Make a well in the centre, add the egg yolks and the iced water and mix with a flat-bladed knife, using a cutting action, until the mixture comes together in beads. Add more water if the dough is too dry. Gently gather the dough together and lift out onto a lightly floured work surface. Press into a ball, cover with plastic wrap and refrigerate for at least 15 minutes.

To make the filling, steam or boil the potato and pumpkin for 10–15 minutes, or until just tender. Drain well and put in a large bowl to cool. Gently fold in the broccoli, cauliflower, zucchini, carrot, spring onion, cheddar, ricotta, parmesan, parsley and beaten egg. Season to taste.

Preheat the oven to 190°C (375°F/Gas 5). Grease six 10 cm (4 inch) pie tins. Divide the pastry into six and roll each portion into a rough 20 cm (8 inch) circle. Place the pastry in the tins, leaving the excess overhanging.

Divide the filling evenly among the pastry cases. Fold over the overhanging pastry, gently folding or pleating as you go. Place on a baking tray, cover and refrigerate for 15 minutes. Bake for 25–30 minutes, or until the pastry is cooked and golden brown. Serve hot.

PREPARATION TIME: 50 MINUTES +   COOKING TIME: 45 MINUTES

CURRIED CHICKEN PIES

PASTRY

375 g (13 oz/3 cups) plain (all-purpose) flour

1 teaspoon ground cumin

1 teaspoon ground turmeric

200 g (7 oz) butter, chopped

2 egg yolks, lightly beaten

100–115 ml ($3^1/_2$–$3^3/_4$ fl oz) iced water

FILLING

50 g ($1^3/_4$ oz) butter

1 onion, chopped

350 g (12 oz) chicken tenderloins, trimmed and finely diced

1 tablespoon curry powder

1 teaspoon cumin seeds

1 tablespoon plain (all-purpose) flour

250 ml (9 fl oz/1 cup) chicken stock

2 tablespoons mango chutney (see Note)

3 tablespoons chopped coriander (cilantro)

milk, to glaze

MAKES 24

To make the pastry, sift the flour, cumin and turmeric into a bowl. Using your fingertips, rub in the butter until the mixture resembles fine breadcrumbs. Make a well in the centre and add the egg yolks and the iced water. Mix with a flat-bladed knife, using a cutting action, until the mixture comes together in beads. Lift onto a lightly floured work surface and gather into a ball. Wrap in plastic wrap and refrigerate for 30 minutes.

Lightly grease two deep 12-hole patty pans or mini muffin tins. Roll out two-thirds of the pastry to 2 mm ($^1/_{16}$ inch) thick, and cut 8 cm ($3^1/_4$ inch) rounds to fit the tins. Roll out the remaining pastry and cut 24 tops with a 5.5 cm ($2^1/_4$ inch) cutter. Chill.

To make the filling, heat the butter in a large saucepan and cook the onion until soft. Add the chicken and, when browned, stir in the curry powder and cumin seeds for 2 minutes. Add the flour and stir for 30 seconds. Remove from the heat and gradually stir in the stock. Return to the heat and stir until the sauce boils and thickens. Reduce the heat and simmer for 2–3 minutes, or until reduced and very thick. Stir in the mango chutney and coriander. Season and cool.

Preheat the oven to 180°C (350°F/Gas 4). Divide the filling equally among the pastry cases and brush the edges with water. Lay the pastry tops over the pies and press around the edges with the tip of a sharp knife. Slash each top to allow steam to escape. Brush with milk and bake for 30 minutes. Cool slightly before removing from the tins. Serve warm.

PREPARATION TIME: 45 MINUTES +   COOKING TIME: 50 MINUTES

NOTE: If the mango pieces in the chutney are quite large, chop them.

LAMB KORMA PIES

PASTRY

375 g (13 oz/3 cups) plain (all-purpose)
flour, sifted
2 tablespoons caraway seeds
180 g (6^1/$_4$ oz) butter, chopped
80 ml (2^1/$_2$ fl oz/^{1}/$_3$ cup) iced water

FILLING

1 tablespoon olive oil
1 small onion, finely chopped
1 garlic clove, crushed
2 tablespoons mild curry paste
250 g (9 oz) lamb fillets, trimmed and
finely diced
1 small potato, finely diced
35 g (1^1/$_4$ oz/^{1}/$_4$ cup) frozen baby peas
60 g (2^1/$_4$ oz/^{1}/$_4$ cup) natural yoghurt

1 egg, lightly beaten, to glaze
2 tablespoons chopped coriander
(cilantro)

MAKES 24

To make the pastry, combine the flour and caraway seeds in a large bowl. Using your fingertips, rub in the butter until the mixture resembles fine breadcrumbs. Make a well in the centre, add the iced water and mix with a flat-bladed knife, using a cutting action, until the mixture comes together in beads. Lift onto a lightly floured work surface and gather into a ball. Flatten slightly into a disc, wrap in plastic wrap and refrigerate for 20 minutes.

To make the filling, heat the oil in a heavy-based saucepan, add the onion and garlic and stir over medium heat for 3–4 minutes, or until the onion is soft. Add the curry paste and stir for 1 minute. Increase the heat to high and add the lamb, potato and peas, stirring for 5 minutes, or until the lamb is well browned all over. Add the yoghurt, bring to the boil, then reduce the heat and simmer, covered, for 30 minutes, or until the lamb is tender. Uncover and simmer for 10 minutes, or until the sauce thickens. Remove from the heat and allow to cool.

Preheat the oven to 180°C (350°F/Gas 5). Lightly grease two 12-hole mini muffin tins. Roll two-thirds of the dough between two sheets of baking paper to 2 mm (^{1}/$_{16}$ inch) thick. Cut 24 rounds with a 7 cm (2^3/$_4$ inch) cutter and ease into the tins. Divide the filling evenly among the pastry cases. Roll out the remaining pastry into a rectangle. Cut 24 strips 1 x 20 cm (^{1}/$_2$ x 8 inches) and twist onto the top of each pie. Brush with the egg and bake for 25–30 minutes, or until golden brown. Cool slightly before removing from the tins. Serve warm, sprinkled with coriander.

PREPARATION TIME: 30 MINUTES +   COOKING TIME: 1 HOUR 20 MINUTES

SPINACH PIE

500 g (1 lb 2 oz) English spinach
1 tablespoon oil
6 spring onions (scallions), finely chopped
125 g (4^1/$_2$ oz) feta cheese, crumbled
90 g (3^1/$_4$ oz/^{3}/$_4$ cup) grated cheddar cheese
5 eggs, lightly beaten
16 sheets filo pastry
80 ml (2^1/$_2$ fl oz/^{1}/$_3$ cup) olive oil
1 egg, extra, lightly beaten, to glaze
1 tablespoon poppy seeds or sesame seeds

SERVES 6–8

Preheat the oven to 210°C (415°F/Gas 6-7). Brush a 25 x 30 cm (10 x 12 inch) ovenproof dish with oil. Wash the spinach thoroughly and shred finely. Put in a large saucepan with just the water that is clinging to the leaves. Cook, covered, over low heat for 2 minutes, or until just wilted. Cool, wring out any excess water and spread out the strands.

Heat the oil in a small frying pan and cook the spring onion for 3 minutes, or until soft. Transfer to a large bowl and add the spinach, cheeses and eggs then season. Stir until the cheeses are distributed evenly. Place one sheet of pastry in the dish, letting the edges overhang. Cover the remaining pastry with a clean, damp tea towel (dish towel) to prevent it drying out. Brush the pastry in the dish with oil. Repeat with another seven layers of pastry, brushing each lightly with oil.

Spread the filling over the pastry, then fold in the edges of the pastry. Brush each remaining sheet of pastry lightly with oil and place on top of the pie. Tuck the edges down the sides, brush the top with egg and sprinkle with poppy seeds. Bake for 35–40 minutes, or until the pastry is golden. Serve immediately.

PREPARATION TIME: 35 MINUTES   COOKING TIME: 40 MINUTES

MINI MEAT PIES

6 sheets ready-rolled shortcrust (pie) pastry
1 tablespoon oil
1 onion, chopped
2 garlic cloves, crushed
500 g (1 lb 2 oz) minced (ground) beef
2 tablespoons plain (all-purpose) flour
375 ml (13 fl oz/1^1/$_2$ cups) beef stock
80 ml (2^1/$_2$ fl oz/^{1}/$_3$ cup) tomato sauce (ketchup)
2 teaspoons worcestershire sauce
^{1}/$_2$ teaspoon dried mixed herbs
2 small tomatoes, sliced
^{1}/$_2$ teaspoon dried oregano leaves

MAKES 24

Preheat the oven to 200°C (400°F/Gas 6). Cut the pastry into 24 circles using a 7 cm (2^3/$_4$ inches) round cutter. Press the circles into two lightly greased 12-hole patty pans or mini muffin tins.

Heat the oil in a heavy-based saucepan, add the onion and garlic and cook over medium heat for 2 minutes, or until the onion is soft. Add the beef and stir over high heat for 3 minutes, or until well browned and all the liquid has evaporated. Use a fork to break up any lumps of meat. Add the flour, stir until combined, then cook over medium heat for 1 minute. Add the stock, sauces and herbs and stir over low heat until boiling. Reduce the heat to low and simmer for 5 minutes until reduced and thickened, stirring occasionally. Allow to cool. Divide the filling among the pastry circles. Top each with two half slices of tomato and sprinkle with oregano. Bake for 25 minutes, or until the pastry is golden brown and crisp. Serve hot.

PREPARATION TIME: 20 MINUTES   COOKING TIME: 25 MINUTES

BEEF PIE

FILLING

2 tablespoons oil

1 kg (2 lb 4 oz) trimmed chuck steak, cubed

1 large onion, chopped

1 large carrot, finely chopped

2 garlic cloves, crushed

2 tablespoons plain (all-purpose) flour

250 ml (9 fl oz/1 cup) beef stock

2 teaspoons thyme

1 tablespoon worcestershire sauce

PASTRY

250 g (9 oz/2 cups) plain (all-purpose) flour

150 g (5$\frac{1}{2}$ oz) chilled butter, cubed

1 egg yolk

2–3 tablespoons iced water

1 egg yolk, to glaze

1 tablespoon milk, to glaze

SERVES 6

Lightly grease a 23 cm (9 inch) pie dish. To make the filling, heat half of the oil in a large frying pan and brown the meat in batches. Remove from the pan. Heat the remaining oil, add the onion, carrot and garlic and brown over medium heat.

Return the meat to the pan and stir in the flour. Cook for 1 minute, then remove from the heat and slowly stir in the stock, mixing the flour in well. Add the thyme and worcestershire sauce and bring to the boil. Season to taste.

Reduce the heat to very low, cover and simmer for 1$\frac{1}{2}$–2 hours, or until the meat is tender. During the last 15 minutes of cooking, remove the lid and allow the liquid to reduce so that the sauce is very thick and suitable for filling a pie. Allow to cool completely.

To make the pastry, sift the flour into a large bowl. Using your fingertips, rub in the butter until it resembles fine breadcrumbs. Add the egg yolk and 2 tablespoons of the water and mix with a flat-bladed knife, using a cutting action, until the mixture comes together in beads. Add more water if the dough is too dry. Turn out onto a lightly floured work surface and gather together to form a smooth dough. Wrap in plastic wrap and refrigerate for 30 minutes.

Preheat the oven to 200°C (400°F/Gas 6). Divide the pastry in half and roll out one piece between two sheets of baking paper until large enough to line the pie dish. Line the dish with the pastry, fill with the cold filling and roll out the remaining pastry to cover the dish. Brush the pastry edges with water. Lay the pastry over the pie and gently press or pinch to seal. Trim any excess pastry. Re-roll the scraps to make decorative shapes and press on the pie.

Cut a few steam holes in the top of the pastry. Beat together the egg yolk and milk and brush over the top of the pie. Bake for 20–30 minutes, or until the pastry is golden and the filling is hot.

PREPARATION TIME: 35 MINUTES +   COOKING TIME: 2 HOURS 45 MINUTES

POTATO PIES

1 kg (2 lb 4 oz) all-purpose potatoes, chopped
1 tablespoon oil
1 onion, finely chopped
1 garlic clove, crushed
500 g (1 lb 2 oz) minced (ground) beef
2 tablespoons plain (all-purpose) flour
500 ml (17 fl oz/2 cups) beef stock
2 tablespoons tomato paste (concentrated purée)
1 tablespoon worcestershire sauce
500 g (1 lb 2 oz) shortcrust (pie) pastry
50 g (1³/4 oz) butter, softened
60 ml (2 fl oz/¹/4 cup) milk

MAKES 6

Steam or boil the potatoes for 10 minutes, or until tender (pierce with the point of a small sharp knife and if the potato comes away easily it is ready). Drain thoroughly, then mash.

Preheat the oven to 210°C (415°F/Gas 6–7). Heat the oil in a frying pan, add the onion and cook for 5 minutes, or until soft. Add the garlic and cook for 1 minute. Add the beef and cook over medium heat for 5 minutes, or until browned, breaking up any lumps with a fork.

Sprinkle the flour over the meat and stir to combine. Add the stock, tomato paste, worcestershire sauce and some salt and pepper to the pan and stir for 2 minutes. Bring to the boil, then reduce the heat slightly and simmer for 5 minutes, or until the mixture has reduced and thickened. Allow to cool completely.

Lightly grease six 11 cm (4¹/4 inch) pie tins. Roll out the pastry between two sheets of baking paper and, using a plate as a guide, cut the pastry into 15 cm (6 inch) circles and line the pie tins. Cut baking paper to cover each tin, spread baking beads or uncooked rice over the paper and bake for 7 minutes. Remove the paper and beads and cook the pastry for another 5 minutes. Allow to cool.

Divide the meat filling equally among the pastry cases. Stir the butter and milk into the mashed potato and pipe or spread all over the top of the meat filling. Bake for 20 minutes, or until the potato is lightly golden.

PREPARATION TIME: 25 MINUTES   COOKING TIME: 1 HOUR 5 MINUTES

LAMB AND FILO PIE

2 tablespoons oil
2 onions, chopped
1 garlic clove, chopped
1 teaspoon ground cumin
1 teaspoon ground coriander
$1/2$ teaspoon ground cinnamon
1 kg (2 lb 4 oz) minced (ground) lamb
3 tablespoons chopped flat-leaf (Italian) parsley
2 tablespoons chopped mint
1 tablespoon tomato paste (concentrated purée)
10 sheets filo pastry
250 g (9 oz) butter, melted

SERVES 6

Heat the oil in a large frying pan. Add the onion and garlic and cook for 3 minutes, or until just soft. Add the cumin, coriander and cinnamon to the pan and cook, stirring continuously, for 1 minute.

Add the lamb to the pan and cook over medium heat for 10 minutes, or until the meat is brown and all the liquid has evaporated. Use a fork to break up any lumps of meat. Add the herbs, tomato paste and $1/4$ teaspoon salt and mix well. Allow to cool completely.

Preheat the oven to 180°C (350°F/Gas 4). Lightly grease a 23 x 33 cm (9 x 13 inch) ovenproof dish. Remove three sheets of filo. Cover the remainder with a damp tea towel (dish towel) to prevent them drying out. Brush the top sheet of filo with melted butter. Cover with another two sheets of filo and brush the top one with butter. Line the ovenproof dish with these sheets, leaving the excess overhanging the dish.

Spread the lamb mixture over the pastry and fold the overhanging pastry over the filling. Butter two sheets of filo, place one on top of the other and fold in half. Place over the top of the filling and tuck in the edges. Butter the remaining sheets of filo, cut roughly into squares and then scrunch these over the top of the pie. Bake for 40 minutes, or until crisp and golden.

PREPARATION TIME: 20 MINUTES   COOKING TIME: 55 MINUTES

FETA AND OLIVE HERB PIE

PASTRY
2 teaspoons sugar

2 teaspoons dried yeast

1 tablespoon olive oil

60 g (2^1/4 oz/^{1}/2 cup) plain (all-purpose)
flour

125 g (4^1/2 oz/1 cup) self-raising flour

FILLING
1 tablespoon olive oil

1 onion, sliced

15 g (^{1}/2 oz) flat-leaf (Italian) parsley,
chopped

1 rosemary sprig, chopped

3 thyme sprigs, chopped

5 basil leaves, torn

40 g (1^1/2 oz/^{1}/4 cup) pine nuts, toasted
(see Note)

1 garlic clove, crushed

175 g (6 oz) feta cheese, crumbled

30 g (1 oz) pitted olives, chopped

SERVES 4–6

Dissolve half the sugar in 125 ml (4 fl oz/^{1}/2 cup) warm water and sprinkle the yeast over the top. Leave in a warm, draught-free place for 10 minutes, or until bubbles appear on the surface. If your yeast doesn't foam, it is dead and you will have to start again. Mix the yeast mixture with the oil.

Sift the flours and ^{1}/2 teaspoon salt into a large bowl. Make a well in the centre and pour in the yeast mixture. Mix well and knead on a lightly floured board until smooth. Cut the dough in half, then roll each half into a 20 cm (8 inch) circle. Place one circle on a lightly greased baking tray, the other on a baking tray covered with baking paper. Cover the circles with a cloth and put in a warm place for 10-15 minutes, or until doubled in size. Preheat the oven to 200°C (400°F/Gas 6).

To make the filling, heat the oil in a frying pan and cook the onion for 10 minutes, or until golden brown. Sprinkle with the remaining sugar and cook for a further 5 minutes, or until caramelized. Transfer to a bowl and mix with the herbs, pine nuts, garlic, feta and olives. Spread the mixture over the pastry on the greased tray. Brush the edge with water and put the second pastry circle on top, using the paper to help lift it over. Press the edges together to seal and pinch together to form a pattern. Cut a few slits in the top of the pastry to allow steam to escape. Bake for 30–35 minutes, or until crisp and golden brown. Serve warm, cut into wedges.

PREPARATION TIME: 40 MINUTES +   COOKING TIME: 45 MINUTES

NOTE: To toast pine nuts, you can dry-fry them in a frying pan, stirring and watching them constantly so they don't burn.

FILO RISOTTO PIE

2 large red capsicums (peppers)

RISOTTO
250 ml (9 fl oz/1 cup) white wine
1 litre (35 fl oz/4 cups) vegetable stock
2 tablespoons oil
1 garlic clove, crushed
1 leek, white part only, sliced
1 fennel bulb, thinly sliced
440 g (15^1/2 oz/2 cups) arborio rice
60 g (2^1/4 oz) freshly grated parmesan cheese

10 sheets filo pastry
60 ml (2 fl oz/^{1}/4 cup) olive oil
500 g (1 lb 2 oz) English spinach, blanched
250 g (9 oz) feta cheese, sliced
1 tablespoon sesame seeds

SERVES 8

Cut the capsicums in half. Remove the seeds and membrane and then cut into large, flattish pieces. Grill (broil) until the skin blackens and blisters. Place on a cutting board, cover with a tea towel (dish towel) and allow to cool. Peel the capsicum and cut the flesh into smaller pieces.

To make the risotto, put the wine and stock into a large saucepan. Bring to the boil and reduce the heat.

Heat the oil and garlic in a large heavy-based saucepan. Add the leek and fennel, cook over medium heat for 5 minutes, or until lightly browned. Add the rice and stir for 3 minutes, or until the rice is translucent.

Add 250 ml (9 fl oz/1 cup) of the stock mixture to the rice and stir constantly until the liquid is absorbed. Continue adding liquid, 125 ml (4 fl oz/^{1}/2 cup) at a time, stirring constantly until all the stock mixture has been used and the rice is tender. (This will take about 40 minutes.) Make sure the liquid stays hot as the risotto will become gluggy if it isn't. Remove from the heat, stir in the parmesan and season. Set aside until cooled slightly.

Brush each sheet of filo with olive oil and fold in half lengthways. Arrange like overlapping spokes on a wheel, in a 23 cm (9 inch) spring-form pan, with one side of the pastry hanging over the side of tin.

Preheat the oven to 180°C (350°F/Gas 4). Spoon half the risotto mixture over the pastry and top with half the red capsicum, half the spinach and half the feta. Repeat with the remaining risotto, capsicum, spinach and feta.

Fold the pastry over the filling, brush lightly with oil and sprinkle with sesame seeds. Bake for 50 minutes, or until the pastry is crisp and golden and the pie is heated through.

PREPARATION TIME: 45 MINUTES   COOKING TIME: 1 HOUR 45 MINUTES

CHEESE AND MUSHROOM PIES

40 g (1½ oz) butter
2 garlic cloves, crushed
500 g (1 lb 2 oz) button mushrooms, sliced
1 small red capsicum (pepper), seeded, membrane removed and finely chopped
165 g (5¾ oz/⅔ cup) sour cream
3 teaspoons wholegrain mustard
70 g (2½ oz/½ cup) finely grated gruyère or cheddar cheese
6 sheets ready-rolled puff pastry
70 g (2½ oz/½ cup) finely grated gruyère or cheddar cheese, extra
1 egg, lightly beaten, to glaze

MAKES 6

Preheat the oven to 190°C (375°F/Gas 5). Lightly grease two baking trays with melted butter or oil. Heat the butter in a large frying pan. Add the garlic and mushroom and cook over medium heat, stirring occasionally, until the mushroom is tender and the liquid has evaporated. Remove from the heat and cool. Stir in the red capsicum.

Combine the sour cream, mustard and cheese. Cut twelve circles with a 14 cm (5½ inch) diameter from the pastry. Spread the cream mixture over six of the circles, leaving a 1 cm (½ inch) border. Top each with mushroom mixture. Sprinkle each with 2 teaspoons of the extra cheese. Brush the outer edges with beaten egg then place the reserved pastry rounds on top of the filling, sealing the edges with a fork. Brush the tops of the pastry with egg. Sprinkle the remaining cheese over the pastry. Place the pies on oven trays and bake for 20 minutes, or until lightly browned and puffed.

PREPARATION TIME: 40 MINUTES   COOKING TIME: 30 MINUTES

FREE-FORM PRAWN PIES

1 kg (2 lb 4 oz) raw prawns (shrimp)
2 cups (250 g/9 oz) plain (all-purpose) flour
125 g (4½ oz) chilled butter, cubed
60 ml (2 fl oz/¼ cup) iced water
1 tablespoon oil
5 cm (2 inch) piece fresh ginger, grated
3 garlic cloves, crushed
80 ml (2½ fl oz/⅔ cup) sweet chilli sauce
80 ml (2½ fl oz/⅔ cup) lime juice
80 ml (2½ fl oz/⅔ cup) thick (double) cream
25 g (1 oz) chopped coriander (cilantro)
1 egg yolk, lightly beaten, to glaze
lime zest strips, to garnish

SERVES 4

Peel the prawns and gently pull out the dark vein from each prawn back, starting from the head end. Sift the flour into a large bowl. Using your fingertips, rub in the butter until the mixture resembles fine breadcrumbs. Make a well in the centre, add the water and mix with a flat-bladed knife, using a cutting action, until the mixture comes together in beads. Gather the dough together and lift out onto a lightly floured surface. Press into a ball and flatten into a disc. Wrap in plastic wrap and chill for 15 minutes. Preheat the oven to 200°C (400°F/Gas 6).

Heat the oil in a large frying pan and fry the ginger, garlic and prawns for 2–3 minutes. Remove the prawns and set aside. Add the chilli sauce, lime juice and cream to the pan and simmer over medium heat, until the sauce has reduced by about one-third. Return the prawns to the pan and add the coriander. Cool. Grease two baking trays. Divide the pastry into four and roll out each portion, between sheets of baking paper, into a 20 cm (8 inch) circle. Divide the filling into four and place a portion in the centre of each pastry circle, leaving a wide border. Fold the edges loosely over the filling. Brush the pastry with egg yolk. Bake for 25 minutes, or until golden. Serve garnished with lime zest.

PREPARATION TIME: 20 MINUTES   COOKING TIME: 30 MINUTES

HARVEST PIE

PASTRY

125 g (4¹/₂ oz) butter, chopped

250 g (9 oz/2 cups) plain (all-purpose) flour

60 ml (2 fl oz/¹/₄ cup) iced water

FILLING

1 tablespoon oil

1 onion, finely chopped

1 small red capsicum (pepper), seeded, membrane removed and chopped

1 small green capsicum (pepper), seeded, membrane removed and chopped

150 g (5¹/₂ oz) pumpkin (winter squash), chopped

1 small potato, chopped

100 g (3¹/₂ oz) broccoli, cut into small florets

1 carrot, chopped

50 g (1³/₄ oz) butter

30 g (1 oz/¹/₄ cup) plain (all-purpose) flour, extra

250 ml (9 fl oz/1 cup) milk

2 egg yolks

60 g (2¹/₄ oz/¹/₂ cup) grated cheddar cheese

1 egg, lightly beaten, to glaze

SERVES 6

Preheat the oven to 180°C (350°F/Gas 4).

To make the pastry, sift the flour into a large bowl. Using your fingertips, rub in the butter until the mixture resembles fine breadcrumbs. Add almost all the water and mix with a flat-bladed knife, using a cutting action until the mixture forms a firm dough, adding more water if necessary. Turn onto a lightly floured work surface and press together until smooth.

Divide the dough in half, roll out one portion and line a deep 21 cm (8¹/₄ inch) fluted flan (tart) tin. Refrigerate for 20 minutes. Roll the remaining pastry out to a 25 cm (10 inch) diameter circle. Cut into strips and lay half of them on a sheet of baking paper, leaving a 1 cm (¹/₂ inch) gap between each strip. Interweave the remaining strips to form a lattice pattern. Cover with plastic wrap and refrigerate, keeping flat, until firm.

Cut a sheet of baking paper to cover the pastry-lined tin. Spread a layer of baking beads or uncooked rice over the paper. Bake for 10 minutes, remove from the oven and discard the paper and beads. Bake for another 10 minutes, or until lightly golden. Allow to cool.

To make the filling, heat the oil in a frying pan. Add the onion and cook for 2 minutes, or until soft. Add the capsicum and cook, stirring, for 3 minutes. Steam or boil the remaining vegetables until just tender. Drain and cool. Mix the onion, capsicum and other vegetables in a large bowl.

Heat the butter in a small saucepan. Add the flour and cook, stirring, for 2 minutes. Add the milk gradually, stirring until smooth between each addition. Stir constantly over medium heat until the mixture boils and thickens. Boil for 1 minute and then remove from the heat. Add the egg yolks and cheese and stir until smooth. Pour the sauce over the vegetables and stir to combine. Pour the mixture into the pastry case and brush the edges with egg. Using the baking paper to lift, invert the pastry lattice over the vegetables, remove the paper, trim the pastry edges and brush with a little beaten egg, sealing it to the cooked pastry. Brush the top with egg and bake for 30 minutes, or until golden brown.

PREPARATION TIME: 40 MINUTES +   COOKING TIME: 1 HOUR

SILVERBEET PIE

PASTRY

250 g (9 oz/2 cups) plain (all-purpose) flour

80 g (2³/4 oz/¹/2 cup) wholemeal (wholewheat) plain (all-purpose) flour

125 g (4¹/2 oz) butter, chopped

80 ml (2¹/2 fl oz/¹/3 cup) iced water

FILLING

800 g (1 lb 12 oz) silverbeet (Swiss chard)

70 g (2¹/2 oz/¹/2 cup) chopped pistachio nuts

40 g (1¹/2 oz/¹/3 cup) chopped raisins

35 g (1¹/4 oz/¹/3 cup) freshly grated parmesan cheese

60 g (2¹/4 oz/¹/2 cup) grated cheddar cheese

3 eggs

170 ml (5¹/2 fl oz/²/3 cup) pouring (whipping) cream

¹/4 teaspoon freshly grated nutmeg

1 egg, extra, lightly beaten, to glaze

SERVES 6–8

To make the pastry, sift the flours into a large bowl. Using your fingertips, rub in the butter for 2 minutes, or until the mixture resembles fine breadcrumbs. Add almost all the water and mix with a flat-bladed knife, using a cutting action, until the mixture forms a firm dough. Add more water if the dough is too dry. Turn the dough onto a lightly floured work surface and press together until smooth. Roll out two-thirds of the pastry and line a greased 23 cm (9 inch) pie dish. Wrap the remaining pastry in plastic wrap and refrigerate both for 20 minutes. Preheat the oven to 180°C (350°F/Gas 4).

To make the filling, remove the stems from the silverbeet and wash the leaves thoroughly. Shred finely. Steam or microwave for 3 minutes, or until tender. Cool, squeeze thoroughly to remove any excess moisture and spread out to dry in separate strands.

Sprinkle the pistachios onto the pastry base. Combine the silverbeet, raisins and cheeses and spread over the pistachios. Whisk the eggs with the cream and nutmeg and pour over the silverbeet mixture.

Roll out the remaining pastry to cover the top of the pie and trim the edges with a sharp knife. Press the edges together to seal. Brush the pie top with the beaten egg and decorate with pastry trimmings. Bake for 45 minutes, or until golden. Serve warm.

PREPARATION TIME: 40 MINUTES +   COOKING TIME: 50 MINUTES

NOTE: This pie is best eaten on the day it is made.

FRUIT MINCE PIES

FRUIT MINCE

40 g (1½ oz/⅓ cup) raisins, chopped

60 g (2¼ oz/⅓ cup) soft brown sugar

30 g (1 oz/¼ cup) sultanas (golden raisins)

50 g (1¾ oz/¼ cup) mixed peel (mixed candied citrus peel)

1 tablespoon currants

1 tablespoon chopped almonds

1 small apple, grated

1 teaspoon lemon juice

½ teaspoon finely grated orange zest

½ teaspoon finely grated lemon zest

½ teaspoon mixed (pumpkin pie) spice

pinch freshly grated nutmeg

25 g (1 oz) unsalted butter, melted

1 tablespoon brandy

PASTRY

250 g (9 oz/2 cups) plain (all-purpose) flour

150 g (5½ oz) chilled unsalted butter, cubed

85 g (3 oz/⅔ cup) icing (confectioners') sugar

2–3 tablespoons iced water

icing (confectioners') sugar, extra, to dust

MAKES 24

To make the fruit mince, combine all the ingredients in a bowl, spoon into a sterilized jar and seal. You can use the fruit mince straightaway but the flavours develop if kept for a while. Keep it in a cool dark place for up to 3 months. (Use ready-made fruit mince if you are short of time.)

Preheat the oven to 180°C (350°F/Gas 4). Lightly grease two 12-hole shallow patty pans or mini muffin tins.

To make the pastry, sift the flour into a bowl. Using your fingertips, rub in the butter until the mixture resembles fine breadcrumbs. Stir in the icing sugar and make a well in the centre. Add almost all the water and mix with a flat-bladed knife, using a cutting action, until the mixture comes together in beads. Add the remaining water if the dough is too dry. Turn out onto a lightly floured work surface and gather into a ball. Roll out two-thirds of the pastry and cut out 24 rounds, slightly larger than the holes in the patty pans, with a round fluted cutter. Fit the rounds into the tins.

Divide the fruit mince evenly among the pastry cases. Roll out the remaining pastry, a little thinner than before, and cut 12 rounds with the same cutter. Using a smaller fluted cutter, cut 12 more rounds. Place the large circles on top of half the pies and press the edges to seal. Place the smaller circles on the remainder. Bake for 25 minutes, or until golden. Leave in the tins for 5 minutes, then lift out with a knife and cool on wire racks. Dust lightly with icing sugar.

PREPARATION TIME: 30 MINUTES   COOKING TIME: 25 MINUTES

BERRY PIE

125 g (4$\frac{1}{2}$ oz/1 cup) self-raising flour
125 g (4$\frac{1}{2}$ oz/1 cup) plain (all-purpose) flour
125 g (4$\frac{1}{2}$ oz) chilled unsalted butter, chopped
2 tablespoons caster (superfine) sugar
1 egg, lightly beaten
60–80 ml (2–2$\frac{1}{2}$ fl oz/$\frac{1}{4}$–$\frac{1}{3}$ cup) milk

BERRY FILLING
2 tablespoons cornflour (cornstarch)
2–4 tablespoons caster (superfine) sugar, to taste
1 teaspoon grated orange zest
1 tablespoon orange juice
600 g (1 lb 5 oz) fresh berries (such as boysenberries, blackberries, loganberries, mulberries, raspberries or youngberries)

1 egg yolk, mixed with 1 teaspoon water, to glaze
icing (confectioners') sugar, to dust

SERVES 4–6

To make the pastry, sift the flours into a large bowl. Using your fingertips, rub in the butter until the mixture resembles fine breadcrumbs. Stir in the sugar, then add the egg and almost all the milk. Mix with a flat-bladed knife, using a cutting action, until the mixture comes together in beads. Add more milk if the dough is too dry. Turn out onto a lightly floured surface and gather together into a ball. Divide into two portions and roll each portion out on a sheet of baking paper, making sure one is the right size to fit the top of a 750 ml (26 fl oz/3 cup) pie dish. Cover with plastic wrap and refrigerate for 30 minutes.

To make the berry filling, mix the cornflour, caster sugar, orange zest and juice in a saucepan. Add half the berries to the pan and stir over low heat for 5 minutes, or until the mixture boils and thickens. Remove from the heat and set aside to cool. Add the remaining berries to the pan, pour into the pie dish and smooth the surface with the back of a spoon.

Preheat the oven to 180°C (350°F/Gas 4). Place the pie top over the fruit and trim the edges. Make sure you do not stretch the pastry or it may shrink during baking and fall back into the dish. Using heart-shaped pastry cutters of various sizes, cut out enough hearts from the remaining pastry to cover the pie top. Arrange them on top of the pie, moistening each one with a little water to make it stick.

Brush all over the surface with the egg glaze. Bake for 35–40 minutes, or until the pastry is crisp and golden brown. Dust with icing sugar just before serving. Serve the pie warm or cold.

PREPARATION TIME: 30 MINUTES +   COOKING TIME: 45 MINUTES

NOTE: Use just one variety of berry or a combination if you prefer. If you want to make the pie when the berries are out of season, use frozen berries. Defrost the berries thoroughly, reserving the juice. Add the berries and juice to the filling and omit the orange juice. You can use tinned berries if you drain them well first.

APPLE PIE

FILLING

6 large granny smith apples, peeled,
cored and cut into wedges
2 tablespoons caster (superfine) sugar
1 teaspoon finely grated lemon zest
pinch ground cloves

PASTRY

250 g (9 oz/2 cups) plain (all-purpose)
flour
30 g (1 oz/¼ cup) self-raising flour
150 g (5½ oz) chilled unsalted butter,
cubed
2 tablespoons caster (superfine) sugar
80–100 ml (2½–3½ fl oz) iced water

2 tablespoons marmalade
1 egg, lightly beaten
1 tablespoon sugar

SERVES 6

Lightly grease a 23 cm (9 inch) pie dish.

To make the filling, put the apple in a saucepan with the sugar, lemon zest, cloves and 2 tablespoons water. Cover and cook over low heat for 8 minutes, or until the apples are just tender, shaking the pan occasionally. Drain and cool completely.

To make the pastry, sift the flours into a bowl. Using your fingertips, rub in the butter until the mixture resembles fine breadcrumbs. Stir in the sugar, then make a well in the centre. Add almost all the iced water and mix with a flat-bladed knife, using a cutting action, until the mixture comes together in beads. Add more water if the dough is too dry. Gather together and lift out onto a lightly floured work surface. Press into a ball and divide into two, making one half a little bigger. Cover with plastic wrap and refrigerate for 20 minutes.

Preheat the oven to 200°C (400°F/Gas 6). Roll out the larger piece of pastry between two sheets of baking paper to line the base and side of the pie dish. Line the pie dish with the pastry. Use a small sharp knife to trim away any excess pastry. Brush the marmalade over the base and spoon the apple mixture into the shell. Roll out the other pastry between the baking paper until large enough to cover the pie. Brush water around the rim then lay the pastry top over the pie. Trim off any excess pastry, pinch the edges and cut a few slits in the top to allow steam to escape.

Re-roll the pastry scraps and cut into leaves for decoration. Lightly brush the top with egg, then sprinkle with sugar. Bake for 20 minutes, then reduce the oven temperature to 180°C (350°F/Gas 4) and bake for another 15–20 minutes, or until golden.

PREPARATION TIME: 45 MINUTES +   COOKING TIME: 50 MINUTES

CHERRY PIE

150 g (5½ oz/1¼ cups) plain (all-purpose) flour
30 g (1 oz/¼ cup) icing (confectioners') sugar
100 g (3½ oz) chilled unsalted butter, chopped
60 g (2¼ oz) ground almonds
60 ml (2 fl oz/¼ cup) iced water
2 x 700 g (1 lb 9 oz) jars pitted morello cherries, drained
1 egg, lightly beaten, to glaze
caster (superfine) sugar, to sprinkle
pouring (whipping) cream or ice cream (optional), to serve

SERVES 6–8

To make the pastry, sift the flour and icing sugar into a bowl. Using your fingertips, rub in the butter until the mixture resembles fine breadcrumbs. Stir in the ground almonds, then add almost all the water. Mix with a flat-bladed knife, using a cutting action, until the mixture forms a dough. Add the remaining water if the dough is too dry. Turn the dough onto a lightly floured work surface and gather together into a ball. Roll out on a sheet of baking paper into a circle about 26 cm (10½ inches) in diameter. Flatten slightly, cover with plastic wrap and refrigerate for 20 minutes. Spread the cherries into a 23 cm (9 inch) round pie dish.

Preheat the oven to 200°C (400°F/Gas 6). Cover the pie dish with the pastry and trim the overhanging edge. Roll out the remaining scraps of pastry and use a small sharp knife to cut out decorations. Brush the pastry top all over with beaten egg and arrange the decorations on top. Brush these with beaten egg as well, and then sprinkle lightly with caster sugar. Place the pie dish on a baking tray (the cherry juice may overflow a little) and cook for 35–40 minutes, or until golden brown.

PREPARATION TIME: 25 MINUTES +   COOKING TIME: 40 MINUTES

FARMHOUSE RHUBARB PIE

185 g (6½ oz/1½ cups) plain (all-purpose) flour, sifted
2 tablespoons icing (confectioners') sugar
125 g (4½ oz) chilled unsalted butter, chopped
1 egg yolk
1 tablespoon iced water
220 g (7¾ oz/1 cup) sugar
750 g (1 lb 10 oz) rhubarb, trimmed, leaves discarded and chopped
2 large apples, peeled, cored and chopped
2 teaspoons grated lemon zest
3 pieces preserved ginger, sliced
2 teaspoons sugar
ground cinnamon, to sprinkle

SERVES 6

Sift the flour into a large bowl and add the icing sugar. Using your fingertips, rub in the butter until the mixture resembles fine breadcrumbs. Add the egg yolk and iced water and mix with a flat-bladed knife, using a cutting action, until the dough comes together. Turn onto a lightly floured work surface, gather into a ball, flatten slightly and refrigerate in plastic wrap for 15 minutes. Preheat the oven to 190°C (375°F/Gas 5). Roll the pastry out to a rough 35 cm (14 inch) circle and line a greased 20 cm (8 inch) pie dish, leaving the extra pastry to hang over the edge. Refrigerate while you prepare the filling.

Heat the sugar and 125 ml (4½ fl oz/½ cup) water in a saucepan for 4-5 minutes, or until syrupy. Add the rhubarb, apple, zest and ginger. Cover and simmer for 5 minutes, or until the rhubarb is cooked but still holds its shape. Drain off the liquid and cool the rhubarb. Spoon into the pastry case and sprinkle with the sugar and cinnamon. Fold the overhanging pastry roughly over the fruit. Bake for 40 minutes, or until golden.

PREPARATION TIME: 40 MINUTES +   COOKING TIME: 50 MINUTES

TOURTE DE BLETTES

60 g (2¼ oz/½ cup) sultanas (golden raisins)

2 tablespoons brandy

400 g (14 oz) plain (all-purpose) flour

100 g (3½ oz) icing (confectioners') sugar

250 g (9 oz) unsalted butter, softened and chopped

3 eggs

800 g (1 lb 12 oz) silverbeet (Swiss chard), stalks removed

100 g (3½ oz/⅔ cup) pine nuts, toasted (see Notes)

3 green cooking apples, peeled, cored and thinly sliced

1 teaspoon grated lemon zest

115 g (4 oz) mild goat's cheese

1 egg yolk, to glaze

icing (confectioners') sugar, extra, to dust

SERVES 6–8

Soak the sultanas in the brandy.

To make the pastry, sift the flour and 1 tablespoon of the icing sugar into a large bowl. Using your fingertips, rub in the butter until the mixture resembles fine breadcrumbs. Make a well in the centre, add one egg and mix with a flat-bladed knife, using a cutting action, until the mixture comes together in beads. Add 1 tablespoon water if the mixture is too dry. Gather together and lift onto a lightly floured work surface. Press into a ball and flatten to a disc. Wrap in plastic wrap and refrigerate for 30 minutes.

Preheat the oven to 180°C (350°F/Gas 4). Heat a baking tray in the oven.

Wash the silverbeet and pat dry. Place in a food processor with the two remaining eggs and the remaining icing sugar. Process to chop the silverbeet and combine, but don't overprocess. Transfer to a bowl. Drain the sultanas and add to the bowl with the pine nuts, then season.

Bring the pastry to room temperature, then break into two portions. Roll one half and use to line a 26 cm (10½ inch) loose-based flan (tart) tin.

Peel the apples, slice thinly and toss with the lemon zest. Put the silverbeet mixture on the pastry and top with the crumbled goat's cheese. Spiral the apple slices on top, making one or two layers.

Roll out the remaining pastry and cover the pie. Trim off the excess pastry and seal the edges with a little water. Crimp the edges.

Brush the pie with the egg yolk and bake for 45–50 minutes, or until golden. Cool slightly. Dust with icing sugar. Serve warm or cold.

PREPARATION TIME: 30 MINUTES +   COOKING TIME: 50 MINUTES

NOTES: This is one of the most traditional and favoured desserts of Nice, France. Although the combination may seem strange at first, you will be pleasantly surprised how complementary the flavours are.

To toast pine nuts, you can dry-fry them in a frying pan, stirring and watching them constantly so they don't burn.

RHUBARB LATTICE PIE

RHUBARB FILLING
500 g (1 lb 2 oz) rhubarb, trimmed, leaves discarded
115 g (4 oz/$\frac{1}{2}$ cup) caster (superfine) sugar
5 cm (2 inch) piece orange zest, pith removed
1 tablespoon orange juice
410 g (14$\frac{1}{2}$ oz) tinned pie apples
caster (superfine) sugar, extra, to taste

150 g (5$\frac{1}{2}$ oz/1$\frac{1}{4}$ cups) plain (all-purpose) flour
$\frac{1}{4}$ teaspoon baking powder
90 g (3$\frac{1}{4}$ oz) chilled unsalted butter, cubed
1 tablespoon caster (superfine) sugar
80–100 ml (2$\frac{1}{2}$–3$\frac{1}{2}$ fl oz) iced water
milk, to glaze
raw (demerara) sugar, to decorate

SERVES 4–6

To make the rhubarb filling, preheat the oven to 180°C (350°F/Gas 4). Cut the rhubarb into 3 cm (1$\frac{1}{4}$ inch) lengths and combine in a large casserole dish with the sugar, orange zest and juice. Cover the dish with a lid or foil and bake for 30 minutes, or until the rhubarb is just tender. Drain away any excess juice and discard the zest. Cool, then stir in the apple. Add more sugar to taste.

While the rhubarb is cooking, sift the flour and baking powder into a bowl. Using your fingertips, rub in the butter until the mixture resembles fine breadcrumbs. Stir in the sugar. Make a well in the centre and add almost all the water. Mix with a flat-bladed knife, using a cutting action, until the mixture comes together in beads. Add more water if the dough is too dry. Gather together, wrap in plastic wrap and chill for 20 minutes.

Roll the pastry out between two sheets of baking paper to a 28 cm (11$\frac{1}{4}$ inch) circle. Cut the pastry into 1.5 cm ($\frac{5}{8}$ inch) strips, using a sharp knife or a fluted cutter. Lay half the strips on a sheet of baking paper, leaving a 1 cm ($\frac{1}{2}$ inch) gap between each strip. Interweave the remaining strips to form a lattice. Cover with plastic wrap and refrigerate, flat, for 20 minutes.

Increase the oven to 210°C (415°F/Gas 6–7). Pour the filling into a 20 cm (8 inch) pie dish and smooth the surface. Invert the pastry lattice on the pie, remove the paper and trim the pastry edge. Bake for 10 minutes. Remove from the oven, brush with milk and sprinkle with sugar. Reduce the oven to 180°C (350°F/Gas 4) and bake the pie for 20 minutes, or until the pastry is golden and the filling is bubbling.

PREPARATION TIME: 35 MINUTES +   COOKING TIME: 1 HOUR

LEMON MERINGUE PIE

185 g (6^1/$_2$ oz/1^1/$_2$ cups) plain (all-purpose) flour
2 tablespoons icing (confectioners') sugar
125 g (4^1/$_2$ oz) chilled unsalted butter, chopped
60 ml (2 fl oz/^{1}/$_4$ cup) iced water

FILLING AND TOPPING
30 g (1 oz/^{1}/$_4$ cup) cornflour (cornstarch)
30 g (1 oz/^{1}/$_4$ cup) plain (all-purpose) flour
230 g (8^1/$_2$ oz/1 cup) caster (superfine) sugar
185 ml (6 fl oz/^{3}/$_4$ cup) lemon juice
3 teaspoons grated lemon zest
40 g (1^1/$_2$ oz) unsalted butter, chopped
6 eggs, separated
350 g (12 oz/1^1/$_2$ cups) caster (superfine) sugar, extra
^{1}/$_2$ teaspoon cornflour (cornstarch), extra

SERVES 6

Sift the flour and icing sugar into a large bowl. Using your fingertips, rub in the butter until the mixture resembles fine breadcrumbs. Add almost all the water and mix with a flat-bladed knife, using a cutting action, until the mixture forms a firm dough. Add more liquid if the dough is too dry. Turn onto a lightly floured surface and gather together into a ball. Roll between two sheets of baking paper until large enough to fit a 23 cm (9 inch) pie dish. Line the pie dish with the pastry, trim the edge and refrigerate for 20 minutes. Preheat the oven to 180°C (350°F/Gas 4).

Line the pastry with a sheet of baking paper and spread a layer of baking beads or uncooked rice evenly over the paper. Bake for 10 minutes, then remove the paper and beads. Bake for a further 10 minutes, or until the pastry is lightly golden. Leave to cool.

To make the filling, put the flours and sugar in a saucepan. Whisk in the lemon juice, zest and 375 ml (13 oz/1^1/$_2$ cups) water. Whisk continually over medium heat until the mixture boils and thickens. Reduce the heat and cook for 1 minute, then whisk in the butter and egg yolks, one yolk at a time. Transfer to a bowl, cover the surface with plastic wrap and allow to cool completely.

To make the topping, preheat the oven to 220°C (425°F/Gas 7). Beat the egg whites in a small dry bowl using electric beaters, until soft peaks form. Add the extra sugar gradually, beating constantly until the meringue is thick and glossy. Beat in the extra cornflour. Pour the cold filling into the cold pastry shell. Spread with meringue to cover, forming peaks. Bake for 5–10 minutes, or until lightly browned. Serve hot or cold.

PREPARATION TIME: 1 HOUR +   COOKING TIME: 45 MINUTES

PECAN PIE

SHORTCRUST PASTRY

185 g (6$\frac{1}{2}$ oz/1$\frac{1}{2}$ cups) plain (all-purpose) flour
125 g (4$\frac{1}{2}$ oz) chilled unsalted butter, chopped
2–3 tablespoons chilled water

FILLING

200 g (7 oz/2 cups) pecans
3 eggs, lightly beaten
50 g (1$\frac{3}{4}$ oz) unsalted butter, melted and cooled
140 g (5 oz/$\frac{3}{4}$ cup) soft brown sugar
170 ml (5$\frac{1}{2}$ fl oz/$\frac{2}{3}$ cup) light corn syrup
1 teaspoon natural vanilla extract

SERVES 6

Preheat the oven to 180°C (350°F/Gas 4). Sift the flour into a large bowl. Using your fingertips, rub in the butter until the mixture resembles fine breadcrumbs. Add almost all the water and mix with a flat-bladed knife, using a cutting action, until the mixture comes together in beads. Add more water if the dough is too dry. Turn out onto a lightly floured work surface and gather together into a ball.

Roll out the pastry to a 35 cm (14 inch) round. Line a 23 cm (9 inch) flan (tart) tin with pastry, trim the edges and refrigerate for 20 minutes. Pile the pastry trimmings together, roll out on baking paper to a rectangle about 2 mm ($\frac{1}{16}$ inch) thick, then refrigerate.

Line the pastry-lined tin with a sheet of baking paper and spread a layer of baking beads or uncooked rice evenly over the paper. Bake for 15 minutes, remove the paper and beads and bake for another 15 minutes, or until lightly golden. Cool completely.

Spread the pecans over the pastry base. Whisk together the eggs, butter, sugar, corn syrup, vanilla extract and a pinch of salt until well combined, then pour over the nuts.

Using a fluted pastry wheel or small sharp knife, cut narrow strips from half of the pastry trimmings. Cut out small stars with a biscuit (cookie) cutter from the remaining trimmings. Arrange decoratively over the filling. Bake the pie for 45 minutes, or until firm. Allow to cool completely and serve at room temperature.

PREPARATION TIME: 30 MINUTES +   COOKING TIME: 1 HOUR 15 MINUTES

PUMPKIN PIE

FILLING

500 g (1 lb 2 oz) pumpkin (winter squash), chopped into small chunks

2 eggs, lightly beaten

140 g (5 oz/^{3}/$_4$ cup) soft brown sugar

80 ml (2^1/$_2$ fl oz/^{1}/$_3$ cup) pouring (whipping) cream

1 tablespoon sweet sherry

1 teaspoon ground cinnamon

^{1}/$_2$ teaspoon freshly grated nutmeg

^{1}/$_2$ teaspoon ground ginger

PASTRY

150 g (5^1/$_2$ oz/1^1/$_4$ cups) plain (all-purpose) flour

100 g (3^1/$_2$ oz) unsalted butter, cubed

2 teaspoons caster (superfine) sugar

80 ml (2^1/$_2$ fl oz/^{1}/$_3$ cup) iced water

1 egg yolk, lightly beaten, to glaze

1 tablespoon milk, to glaze

SERVES 8

Lightly grease a 23 cm (9 inch) round pie dish. Steam or boil the pumpkin for 10 minutes, or until just tender. Drain the pumpkin thoroughly, then mash and set aside to cool.

To make the pastry, sift the flour into a large bowl. Using your fingertips, rub in the butter until the mixture resembles fine breadcrumbs. Stir in the caster sugar. Make a well in the centre, add almost all the water and mix with a flat-bladed knife, using a cutting action, until the mixture comes together in beads. Add the remaining water if the dough is too dry.

Gather the dough together and roll out between two sheets of baking paper until large enough to cover the base and side of the pie dish. Line the dish with pastry, trim away the excess pastry and crimp the edges. Roll out the pastry trimmings to 2 mm (^{1}/$_{16}$ inch) thick. Using a sharp knife, cut out leaf shapes of different sizes and score vein markings onto the leaves. Refrigerate the pastry-lined dish and the leaf shapes for about 20 minutes.

Preheat the oven to 180°C (350°F/Gas 4). Cut baking paper to cover the pastry-lined dish. Spread baking beads or uncooked rice over the paper. Bake for 10 minutes, remove the paper and beads and bake for another 10 minutes, or until lightly golden. Meanwhile, place the leaves on a baking tray lined with baking paper, brush with the combined egg yolk and milk and bake for 10–15 minutes, or until lightly golden. Set aside to cool.

To make the filling, whisk the eggs and brown sugar in a large bowl. Add the cooled mashed pumpkin, cream, sherry, cinnamon, nutmeg and ginger and stir to combine thoroughly. Pour the filling into the pastry shell, smooth the surface with the back of a spoon, then bake for 40 minutes, or until set. If the pastry edges begin to brown too much during cooking, cover the edges with foil. Allow the pie to cool to room temperature and then decorate the top with the leaves. Pumpkin pie can be served with ice cream or whipped cream.

PREPARATION TIME: 20 MINUTES +   COOKING TIME: 1 HOUR 10 MINUTES

FREE-FORM BLUEBERRY PIE

185 g (6¹/₂ oz/1¹/₂ cups) plain (all-purpose) flour
60 g (2¹/₄ oz/¹/₂ cup) icing (confectioners') sugar
125 g (4¹/₂ oz) chilled unsalted butter, cubed
60 ml (2 fl oz/¹/₄ cup) lemon juice
500 g (1 lb 2 oz) blueberries
30 g (1 oz/¹/₄ cup) icing (confectioners') sugar, extra
1 teaspoon finely grated lemon zest
¹/₂ teaspoon ground cinnamon
1 egg white, lightly beaten
icing (confectioners') sugar, extra, to dust
whipped cream or ice cream, to serve

SERVES 4

Preheat the oven to 180°C (350°F/Gas 4). Sift the flour and icing sugar into a bowl. Using your fingertips, rub in the butter until the mixture resembles fine breadcrumbs. Make a well in the centre and add almost all the juice. Mix together with a flat-bladed knife, using a cutting action, until the mixture comes together in beads. Add the remaining juice if the dough is too dry.

Gently gather the dough together and lift onto a sheet of baking paper. Roll out to a circle about 30 cm (12 inches) in diameter. Cover with plastic wrap and refrigerate for 10 minutes. Put the blueberries in a bowl and sprinkle them with the icing sugar, lemon zest and cinnamon.

Place the pastry (still on the baking paper) on a baking tray. Brush the centre of the pastry lightly with egg white. Pile the blueberry mixture onto the pastry in a 20 cm (8 inch) diameter circle, then fold the edges of the pastry over the filling, leaving the centre uncovered. Bake for 30–35 minutes. Dust with icing sugar and serve warm with whipped cream or ice cream.

PREPARATION TIME: 20 MINUTES +   COOKING TIME: 35 MINUTES

REAL LEMON PIE

4 thin-skinned lemons, washed well
450 g (1 lb/2 cups) caster (superfine) sugar
220 g (7³/₄ oz/1³/₄ cups) plain (all-purpose) flour
150 g (5¹/₂ oz) chilled unsalted butter, chopped
2 tablespoons caster (superfine) sugar, extra
1–2 tablespoons iced water
4 eggs
milk, to glaze

SERVES 8–10

Slice two lemons very thinly and remove the seeds. Peel the other lemons, removing all the pith, and slice the flesh very thinly. Remove the seeds. Put all the lemons in a bowl with the sugar and stir until all the slices are coated. Cover and leave overnight.

Preheat the oven to 180°C (350°F/Gas 4). Sift the flour and a pinch of salt into a bowl. Using your fingertips, rub in the butter until the mixture resembles fine breadcrumbs. Stir in the extra sugar. Gradually add the iced water and mix with a flat-bladed knife, using a cutting action until the mixture comes together in beads. Gather the dough together, divide in half and roll each portion into a 25 cm (10 inch) circle. Lightly grease a 23 cm (9 inch) pie dish and line with pastry. Cover and refrigerate the other circle. Beat the eggs and add to the lemon slices, mixing gently but thoroughly. Spoon into the pastry shell and cover with the pastry circle, crimping the edges to seal. Decorate the top with pastry scraps, brush with milk and bake for 50–55 minutes, or until golden brown.

PREPARATION TIME: 30 MINUTES +   COOKING TIME: 50–55 MINUTES

BANOFFIE PIE

WALNUT PASTRY

150 g (5½ oz/1¼ cups) plain (all-purpose) flour
2 tablespoons icing (confectioners') sugar
85 g (3 oz/¾ cup) ground walnuts
80 g (2¾ oz) chilled unsalted butter, chopped
2–3 tablespoons iced water

FILLING

400 g (14 oz) tinned condensed milk
30 g (1 oz) unsalted butter
1 tablespoon golden syrup or dark corn syrup
4 bananas, sliced
375 ml (13 fl oz/1½ cups) pouring (whipping) cream, whipped
50 g (1¾ oz) dark chocolate, melted

SERVES 8

To make the walnut pastry, sift the flour and icing sugar into a large bowl and add the walnuts. Using your fingertips, rub in the butter until the mixture resembles fine breadcrumbs. Mix in the iced water with a flat-bladed knife, using a cutting action, until the mixture forms a firm dough. Add more water if the dough is too dry. Turn onto a lightly floured work surface and gather together into a ball. Wrap and refrigerate for 15 minutes. Roll out to fit a 23 cm (9 inch) flan (tart) tin. Refrigerate for 20 minutes.

Preheat the oven to 180°C (350°F/Gas 4). Line the pastry base with baking paper and spread baking beads or uncooked rice over the paper. Bake for 15 minutes, remove the paper and beads and bake for another 10 minutes, or until lightly golden. Set aside to cool completely.

To make the filling, put the condensed milk, butter and golden syrup in a small saucepan. Stir over medium heat for 5 minutes, until it boils and thickens and turns a light caramel colour. Cool slightly, then arrange half the bananas over the pastry and pour the caramel over the top. Smooth the surface and refrigerate for 30 minutes.

Drop spoonfuls of cream over the caramel and arrange the remaining banana on top. Drizzle with melted chocolate.

PREPARATION TIME: 35 MINUTES +   COOKING TIME: 30 MINUTES

LIME CHIFFON PIE

ALMOND PASTRY
150 g (5$\frac{1}{2}$ oz/1$\frac{1}{4}$ cups) plain (all-purpose)
flour
90 g (3$\frac{1}{4}$ oz) ground almonds
90 g (3$\frac{1}{4}$ oz) chilled unsalted butter,
chopped
1–2 tablespoons iced water

FILLING
6 egg yolks
115 g (4 oz/$\frac{1}{2}$ cup) caster (superfine) sugar
100 g (3$\frac{1}{2}$ oz) unsalted butter, melted
80 ml (2$\frac{1}{2}$ fl oz/$\frac{1}{3}$ cup) lime juice
2 teaspoons finely grated lime zest
2 teaspoons powdered gelatine
125 ml (4 fl oz/$\frac{1}{2}$ cup) pouring (whipping)
cream, whipped

110 g (3$\frac{3}{4}$ oz/$\frac{1}{2}$ cup) sugar
zest of 4 limes, finely shredded

SERVES 12

Sift the flour into a large bowl and add the almonds. Using your fingertips, rub in the butter until the mixture resembles fine breadcrumbs. Add almost all the iced water and mix with a flat-bladed knife, using a cutting action, until the mixture forms a firm dough. Add more water if necessary. Turn onto a lightly floured surface and gather together into a ball. Roll the pastry out to fit a 23 cm (9 inch) fluted flan (tart) tin. Line the tin, trim the edges and refrigerate for 20 minutes.

Preheat the oven to 180°C (350°F/Gas 4). Line the pastry-lined tin with a sheet of baking paper and spread a layer of baking beads or uncooked rice evenly over the paper. Bake for 20 minutes, then remove the paper and beads and bake for another 20 minutes, or until lightly golden. Allow to cool completely.

To make the filling, put the egg yolks, caster sugar, butter, lime juice and zest in a heatproof bowl. Whisk to combine thoroughly and dissolve the sugar. Stand the bowl over a saucepan of simmering water, making sure the base of the bowl does not touch the water, and stir constantly for 15 minutes, or until the mixture thickens. Remove from the heat and cool slightly. Put 1 tablespoon water in a small heatproof bowl, sprinkle the gelatine in an even layer over the surface and leave to go spongy. Do not stir. Bring a small saucepan filled with about 4 cm (1$\frac{1}{2}$ inches) water to the boil, remove from the heat and place the bowl into the pan. The water should come halfway up the side of the bowl. Stir the gelatine until clear and dissolved. Cool slightly, add to the lime curd and stir to combine. Cool to room temperature, stirring occasionally.

Fold the cream through the lime curd and pour into the pastry case. Refrigerate for 2–3 hours, until set. Leave the pie for 15 minutes at room temperature before serving.

To prepare the lime zest, combine the sugar with 1 tablespoon water in a small saucepan. Stir over low heat until the sugar has dissolved. Bring to the boil, add the zest and simmer for 3 minutes. Drain the zest on a wire rack, then decorate the lime chiffon pie before serving.

PREPARATION TIME: 30 MINUTES + COOKING TIME: 1 HOUR

CUSTARD PIE

1 vanilla bean, sliced in half lengthways
750 ml (26 fl oz/3 cups) milk
110 g (3³/₄ oz) caster (superfine) sugar
110 g (3³/₄ oz) semolina
1 tablespoon finely grated lemon zest
1 cinnamon stick
40 g (1¹/₂ oz) unsalted butter, cubed
4 large eggs, lightly beaten
12 sheets filo pastry
60 g (2¹/₄ oz) unsalted butter, extra, melted

SYRUP
80 g (2³/₄ oz) caster (superfine) sugar
¹/₂ teaspoon ground cinnamon
1 tablespoon lemon juice
5 cm (2 inch) strip lemon zest

SERVES 6–8

Scrape the vanilla bean seeds into a saucepan. Add the bean, milk, sugar, semolina, lemon zest and cinnamon stick and gently bring to the boil, stirring constantly. Reduce the heat to low and simmer for 2 minutes so the mixture thickens. Remove from the heat. Mix in the butter. Cool for 10 minutes, then remove the cinnamon stick and vanilla bean and gradually mix in the egg. Preheat the oven to 180°C (350°F/Gas 4).

Cover the filo with a damp tea towel (dish towel). Remove a sheet, brush one side with melted butter and place, buttered side down, in a 3 x 20 x 30 cm (1¹/₄ x 8 x 12 inch) baking tin. The filo will overlap the edges. Repeat with five more sheets, buttering one side of each as you go.

Pour the custard over the filo and cover the top with the remaining pastry, brushing each sheet with butter as you go. Brush the top with butter. Using a small sharp knife, trim the pastry to the edges of the tin. Bake for 40–45 minutes, or until the custard has puffed up and set and the pastry is golden brown. Leave to cool.

Mix all the syrup ingredients with 80 ml (2¹/₂ fl oz/¹/₃ cup) water in a saucepan. Slowly bring to the boil, then reduce the heat to low and simmer for 10 minutes. The syrup will thicken. Remove from the heat and cool for 10 minutes. Remove the lemon zest.

If the filo has risen above the edges of the tin, flatten the top layer with your hand then pour the syrup over the pie. This will prevent the syrup running over the sides. Allow to cool again before serving.

PREPARATION TIME: 35 MINUTES +   COOKING TIME: 1 HOUR

QUICHES, TARTS AND FLANS

ASPARAGUS AND ARTICHOKE QUICHE

PASTRY

220 g (7¾ oz/1¾ cups) plain (all-purpose) flour
100 g (3½ oz) chopped chilled butter
2 tablespoons iced water

FILLING

150 g (5½ oz) asparagus spears, woody ends trimmed and cut into bite-sized pieces
3 eggs
125 ml (4 fl oz/½ cup) pouring (whipping) cream
40 g (1½ oz/⅓ cup) grated gruyère cheese
140 g (5 oz) marinated artichoke hearts, quartered
60 g (2¼ oz/½ cup) grated cheddar cheese

SERVES 4–6

To make the pastry, sift the flour into a bowl. Using your fingertips, rub in the butter until the mixture resembles fine breadcrumbs. Make a well in the centre and add the iced water. Mix with a flat-bladed knife, using a cutting action, until the mixture comes together in beads. Add a little more water if the dough is too dry. Turn out onto a lightly floured work surface and gather into a ball. Cover with plastic wrap and refrigerate for 20 minutes.

Preheat the oven to 190°C (375°F/Gas 5). Roll out the pastry between two sheets of baking paper to fit a shallow loose-based 25 cm (10 inch) flan (tart) tin. Lift the pastry into the tin and press it well into the sides. Trim off any excess by rolling a rolling pin across the top of the tin. Refrigerate the pastry for 20 minutes. Cover the shell with baking paper, fill evenly with baking beads or uncooked rice and bake for 15 minutes, or until the pastry is dried out and golden. Remove the paper and beads and cool slightly. Reduce the oven temperature to 180°C (350°F/Gas 4).

To make the filling, blanch the asparagus in a saucepan of boiling salted water. Drain, then refresh in ice-cold water. Lightly beat together the eggs, cream and gruyère, then season. Spread the artichoke hearts over the cooled pastry, along with the asparagus. Pour on the egg and cream mixture and sprinkle with the cheddar. Bake for 25 minutes, or until the filling is set and golden. Cover with foil if the pastry becomes too brown before the filling is fully set.

PREPARATION TIME: 40 MINUTES +   COOKING TIME: 45 MINUTES

HERBED FISH TARTLETS

PASTRY
150 g (5¹/₂ oz/1¹/₄ cups) plain (all-purpose) flour
90 g (3¹/₄ oz) butter, chopped
1 tablespoon chopped thyme
1 tablespoon chopped dill
2 tablespoons chopped flat-leaf (Italian) parsley
90 g (3¹/₄ oz) cheddar cheese, finely grated
60-80 ml (2-2¹/₂ fl oz/¹/₄-¹/₃ cup) iced water

FILLING
400 g (14 oz) skinless firm white fish fillets
2 spring onions (scallions), finely chopped
2 tablespoons chopped parsley
60 g (2¹/₄ oz) cheddar cheese, finely grated
2 eggs
125 ml (4 fl oz/¹/₂ cup) pouring (whipping) cream

MAKES 8

Lightly grease eight 10 cm (4 inch) round fluted flan (tart) tins. Sift the flour into a large bowl. Using your fingertips, rub in the butter until the mixture resembles fine breadcrumbs. Stir in the herbs and cheddar. Make a well in the centre. Add almost all the water and mix with a flat-bladed knife, using a cutting action, until the mixture comes together in beads. Add more water if the dough is too dry. Gather together and form into a ball. Wrap in plastic wrap and refrigerate for 15 minutes.

Preheat the oven to 210°C (415°F/Gas 6-7). Divide the pastry into eight portions. Roll each on a lightly floured work surface, large enough to fit the tins. Ease into the tins, pressing into the sides. Trim the edges with a sharp knife or by rolling a rolling pin across the tops of the tins. Place the tins on a baking tray. Cover each piece of pastry with a sheet of baking paper. Spread a single layer of baking beads or uncooked rice evenly over the base. Bake for 10 minutes, then remove the paper and beads and bake for another 10 minutes, or until lightly browned. Cool.

To make the filling, put the fish in a frying pan and add enough water to cover. Bring to the boil, reduce the heat and simmer gently for 3 minutes. Remove from the pan with a slotted spoon and drain on crumpled paper towel. Allow to cool, then flake with a fork. Divide among the cases and sprinkle with the combined spring onion, parsley and cheddar. Whisk together the eggs and cream, then pour over the fish. Bake for 25 minutes, or until set and golden brown. Serve immediately.

PREPARATION TIME: 40 MINUTES + COOKING TIME: 45 MINUTES

NOTE: Smoked fish can be used. You can make the recipe in a 23 cm (9 inch) flan (tart) tin. Cooking time may be longer but check after 25 minutes.

SWEET ONION TARTS

PASTRY
125 g (4$\frac{1}{2}$ oz/1 cup) plain (all-purpose) flour
80 g (2$\frac{3}{4}$ oz) butter, chopped
1 tablespoon bottled green peppercorns, drained
1 egg yolk
1 teaspoon dijon mustard
2 teaspoons iced water

SWEET ONION FILLING
2 tablespoons olive oil
3 onions, sliced
1 garlic clove, sliced
2 teaspoons sugar
2 tablespoons balsamic vinegar
40 g (1$\frac{1}{2}$ oz/$\frac{1}{3}$ cup) raisins

1 tablespoon olive paste
80 g (2$\frac{3}{4}$ oz) feta cheese

MAKES 20

Lightly grease 20 holes in two 12-hole patty pans or mini muffin tins. Sift the flour and $\frac{1}{4}$ teaspoon salt into a bowl. Using your fingertips, rub in the butter until the mixture resembles fine breadcrumbs. Make a well in the centre. Crush the peppercorns with the back of a knife and chop finely. Add to the flour with the egg yolk, mustard and the iced water. Mix with a flat-bladed knife, using a cutting action, until the mixture comes together in beads. Turn onto a lightly floured work surface and press together into a ball. Wrap in plastic wrap and refrigerate for 20 minutes.

Preheat the oven to 200°C (400°F/Gas 6). Roll the dough out on a lightly floured work surface to 2–3 mm ($\frac{1}{16}$–$\frac{1}{8}$ inch). Cut 20 rounds with an 8 cm (3$\frac{1}{4}$ inch) cutter. Put in the patty pans and prick with a fork. Bake for 8–10 minutes, or until golden.

To make the filling, heat the oil in a heavy-based saucepan. Add the onion and garlic and cook, covered, over low heat for 30 minutes, or until the onion is very soft and beginning to brown. Increase the heat to moderate, add the sugar and vinegar and cook, stirring, until most of the liquid has evaporated and the onion is glossy. Stir in the raisins.

Spread a little olive paste into the base of each pastry case. Spoon the onion mixture over it and crumble the feta on top. Serve warm or at room temperature.

PREPARATION TIME: 30 MINUTES +   COOKING TIME: 40 MINUTES

SEAFOOD QUICHE

2 sheets ready-rolled shortcrust (pie) pastry
100 g (3½ oz) scallops
30 g (1 oz) butter
100 g (3½ oz) raw prawn meat
100 g (3½ oz) tinned, fresh or frozen crabmeat, drained
90 g (3¼ oz) cheddar cheese, grated
3 eggs
1 tablespoon plain (all-purpose) flour
125 ml (4 fl oz/½ cup) pouring (whipping) cream
125 ml (4 fl oz/½ cup) milk
1 small fennel bulb, finely sliced
1 tablespoon grated parmesan cheese

SERVES 4–6

Lightly grease a 22 cm (8½ inch) diameter loose-based flan (tart) tin. Place the two sheets of pastry slightly overlapping, on a flat surface, and roll out until large enough to fit the prepared tin. Press the pastry into the base and side of the tin and trim off any excess with a sharp knife. Refrigerate for 20 minutes.

Slice or pull off any vein, membrane or hard white muscle from the scallops, leaving any roe attached. Preheat the oven to 190°C (375°F/Gas 5).

Cover the pastry with baking paper, fill evenly with baking beads or uncooked rice and bake for 10 minutes. Remove the paper and beads and bake for another 10 minutes, or until lightly golden. Cool on a wire rack. If the pastry puffs up, press down lightly with a tea towel (dish towel).

Melt the butter in a frying pan and fry the prawns and scallops for 2–3 minutes, or until cooked. Allow to cool, then arrange all the seafood over the base of the pastry shell. Sprinkle with the cheddar.

Beat the eggs, whisk in the flour, cream and milk and season. Pour over the filling. Sprinkle with fennel and parmesan. Bake for 30–35 minutes, or until set and golden brown. Cool slightly before serving.

PREPARATION TIME: 20 MINUTES +   COOKING TIME: 1 HOUR

TOMATO AND OLIVE FLAN

PASTRY

250g (9 oz/2 cups) plain (all-purpose) flour
90 g (3¼ oz) butter, chopped
1 egg yolk combined with 1 tablespoon water

FILLING

6 small tomatoes
2 tablespoons olive oil
1–2 tablespoons French mustard
15 g (½ oz) butter
3 large onions, thinly sliced
1 teaspoon sugar
2 tablespoons shredded basil
125 g (4½ oz/1 cup) pitted black olives, sliced
135 g (4¾ oz/1 cup) grated gruyère cheese

SERVES 4–6

Preheat the oven to 210°C (415°F/Gas 6-7). Brush a deep 20 cm (8 inch) flan (tart) tin with melted butter or oil. Coat the base and sides of the tin evenly with flour and shake off any excess.

To make the pastry, put the flour and butter in a food processor and process for 30 seconds, or until the mixture reaches a fine crumbly texture. Add the combined egg yolk and water and process for 30 seconds or until the mixture comes together. Gather together on a lightly floured work surface. Wrap in plastic wrap and refrigerate for 30 minutes.

To make the filling, score a cross in the base of each tomato. Put in a heatproof bowl and cover with boiling water. Leave for 30 seconds, then transfer to cold water, drain and peel away the skin from the cross. Cut the tomatoes in half, scoop out the seeds and chop the flesh. Mix together the oil and French mustard to make a smooth paste.

Roll the pastry out to fit the prepared tin. Cover the pastry with a large sheet of baking paper. Spread a layer of baking beads or uncooked rice over the paper. Bake for 15 minutes, remove from the oven, discard the paper and beads and leave the pastry to cool.

Spread the mustard and oil mixture over the pastry base. Heat the butter in a frying pan and cook the tomato and onion until soft. Remove from the heat. Drain off the excess liquid. Spoon the tomato over the mustard and oil mixture. Mix together the sugar, basil and olives and sprinkle over the tomato mixture. Top with the gruyère. Bake for 20 minutes, or until the pastry is crisp and the cheese browned.

PREPARATION TIME: 40 MINUTES +   COOKING TIME: 45 MINUTES

CHERRY TOMATO AND PESTO TART

500 g (1 lb 2 oz) block puff pastry, thawed
125 g (4½ oz/½ cup) ready-made pesto
375 g (13 oz) cherry tomatoes
2 spring onions (scallions), finely sliced
extra virgin olive oil, to drizzle
spring onion (scallion) slices, to garnish

SERVES 4

Divide the pastry into two portions. Roll each portion between two sheets of baking paper. If making four tartlets, cut out two 12 cm (4½ inch) circles of pastry from each portion, or for two long tartlets roll each portion of pastry into a rectangle 12 x 25 cm (4½ x 10 inches).

Preheat the oven to 200°C (400°F/Gas 6). Spread the pesto over the pastry shapes, leaving a 1.5 cm (5/8 inch) border. Top with the cherry tomatoes and finely sliced spring onion. Season and bake for 10 minutes, or until golden. Drizzle with extra virgin olive oil and garnish with the spring onion slices. Serve warm or hot.

PREPARATION TIME: 15 MINUTES   COOKING TIME: 10 MINUTES

TAPENADE AND ANCHOVY TARTLETS

500 g (1 lb 2 oz) block puff pastry, thawed
125 g (4½ oz/½ cup) ready-made tapenade
50 g (1¾ oz) tinned anchovies, drained
35 g (1¼ oz/⅓ cup) freshly grated parmesan cheese
80 g (2¾ oz/½ cup) grated mozzarella cheese

SERVES 4

Divide the pastry into two portions. Roll each portion between two sheets of baking paper. If making four tartlets, cut out two 12 cm (4½ inch) circles of pastry from each portion, or for two long tartlets roll each portion of pastry into a rectangle 12 x 25 cm (4½ x 10 inches).

Preheat the oven to 200°C (400°F/Gas 6). Spread the tapenade evenly over the pastry shapes, leaving a 1.5 cm (5/8 inch) border. Cut the anchovies into thin strips and arrange them over the top of the tapenade. Sprinkle the parmesan and mozzarella over the top. Bake for 10 minutes, or until risen and golden.

PREPARATION TIME: 15 MINUTES   COOKING TIME: 10 MINUTES

SMOKED COD FLAN

PASTRY

125 g (4¹/₂ oz/1 cup) plain (all-purpose) flour
60 g (2¹/₄ oz) butter, chopped
1 egg, lightly beaten
1 tablespoon lemon juice
1–2 tablespoons iced water

FILLING

300 g (10¹/₂ oz) smoked cod or haddock fillets
3 eggs, lightly beaten
125 ml (4 fl oz/¹/₂ cup) pouring (whipping) cream
60 g (2¹/₄ oz) cheddar cheese, grated
1 tablespoon chopped dill

SERVES 6

Preheat the oven to 210°C (415°F/Gas 6–7). Lightly grease a 22 cm (8¹/₂ inch) diameter loose-based fluted flan (tart) tin.

Sift the flour into a large bowl. Using your fingertips, rub in the butter until the mixture resembles fine breadcrumbs. Make a well in the centre and add the egg, lemon juice and most of the iced water. Mix with a flat-bladed knife, using a cutting action, until the mixture comes together in beads. Add more water if the dough is too dry. Gently gather the dough together into a ball, flatten into a disc and wrap in plastic wrap. Refrigerate for 20 minutes.

Roll out the dough between two sheets of baking paper until large enough to cover the base and side of the tin. Remove the top sheet of paper and put the pastry in the tin, pressing into the sides. Line with baking paper large enough to cover the base and sides and spread a layer of baking beads or uncooked rice over the top. Bake for 10 minutes, remove the paper and beads and bake for another 5 minutes, or until golden. Remove and cool slightly. Reduce the oven to 180°C (350°F/Gas 4).

To make the filling, put the cod in a frying pan and cover with water. Bring to the boil, reduce the heat and simmer for 10–15 minutes, or until the cod flakes easily when tested with a fork. Drain on crumpled paper towel, then allow to cool.

Flake the cod into small pieces, using a fork. Combine the eggs, cream, cheddar and dill in a bowl, add the cod and mix well. Spoon into the pastry shell and bake for 40 minutes, or until set. Serve the flan hot or cold with lemon or lime wedges and a green salad.

PREPARATION TIME: 30 MINUTES +   COOKING TIME: 55 MINUTES

ROCKET, BASIL AND LEEK QUICHE

150 g (5$\frac{1}{2}$ oz) rocket (arugula), stalks removed

185 g (6$\frac{1}{2}$ oz/1$\frac{1}{2}$ cups) plain (all-purpose) flour

125 g (4$\frac{1}{2}$ oz) butter, chopped

1–2 tablespoons iced water

1 tablespoon oil

1 large leek, white part only, thinly sliced

2 garlic cloves, crushed

2 eggs

125 ml (4 fl oz/$\frac{1}{2}$ cup) milk

125 ml (4 fl oz/$\frac{1}{2}$ cup) pouring (whipping) cream

basil leaves, to garnish

parmesan cheese shavings, to garnish (optional)

SERVES 4–6

Preheat the oven to 210°C (415°F/Gas 6–7). Wash the rocket and shake off the excess water. Finely slice the rocket leaves.

Sift the flour into a bowl. Using your fingertips, rub in the butter until the mixture resembles fine breadcrumbs. Add the iced water and mix to a soft dough with a flat-bladed knife, using a cutting action. Turn onto a lightly floured work surface and knead for 10 seconds, or until smooth. Refrigerate, covered in plastic wrap, for 30 minutes.

Roll the pastry, between two sheets of plastic wrap, large enough to cover the base and side of a shallow 23 cm (9 inch) flan (tart) tin. Cover the pastry-lined tin with a sheet of baking paper and spread baking beads or uncooked rice over the paper. Bake for 10 minutes, remove the paper and beads and bake for another 5 minutes or until lightly golden. Reduce the heat to 180°C (350°F/Gas 4).

Heat the oil in a frying pan, add the leek and garlic and stir over low heat for 5 minutes or until the leek is soft. Add the rocket and stir over heat for 1 minute. Remove from the heat and allow to cool. Spread over the base of the pastry shell. Combine the eggs, milk and cream and whisk until smooth. Pour into the pastry shell. Bake for 50 minutes, or until set and golden. Serve topped with basil leaves and shaved parmesan, if desired.

PREPARATION TIME: 30 MINUTES +   COOKING TIME: 1 HOUR 10 MINUTES

BLUE CHEESE
AND ONION FLAN

2 tablespoons olive oil

1 kg (2 lb 4 oz) red onions, very thinly sliced

1 teaspoon soft brown sugar

185 g (6^1/$_2$ oz/1^1/$_2$ cups) plain (all-purpose) flour

100 g (3^1/$_2$ oz) chilled butter, cubed

60–80 ml (2–2^1/$_2$ fl oz/^{1}/$_4$–^{1}/$_3$ cup) iced water

185 ml (6 fl oz/^{3}/$_4$ cup) pouring (whipping) cream

3 eggs

100 g (3^1/$_2$ oz) blue cheese, crumbled

1 teaspoon chopped thyme leaves

SERVES 8

Heat the oil in a heavy-based frying pan over low heat and cook the onion and sugar, stirring, for 45 minutes, or until the onion is caramelized.

Sift the flour into a large bowl. Using your fingertips, rub in the butter until the mixture resembles fine breadcrumbs. Make a well in the centre and add the iced water. Mix with a flat-bladed knife, using a cutting action, until the mixture comes together in beads. Gently gather together and lift onto a lightly floured work surface. Press into a ball, wrap in plastic wrap and refrigerate for 30 minutes.

Preheat the oven to 180°C (350°F/Gas 4). Roll out the pastry on a lightly floured surface to fit a lightly greased 22 cm (8^1/$_2$ inch) round loose-based flan (tart) tin. Invert the pastry over the tin and press in, allowing the excess to hang over the side. Trim any excess pastry, then refrigerate for 10 minutes. Line the pastry shell with baking paper and fill with baking beads or uncooked rice. Bake on a baking tray for 10 minutes, remove the paper and beads and bake for another 10 minutes, or until lightly golden and dry.

Cool, then gently spread the onion mixture over the base of the pastry. Whisk the cream in a bowl with the eggs, blue cheese, thyme and some pepper. Pour over the onion and bake for 35 minutes, or until firm.

PREPARATION TIME: 40 MINUTES +   COOKING TIME: 1 HOUR 40 MINUTES

CRAB QUICHE

PASTRY

220 g (7³/4 oz/1³/4 cups) plain
(all-purpose) flour
100 g (3¹/2 oz) chilled butter, chopped
2 tablespoons iced water

FILLING

20 g (³/4 oz) butter
1 onion, thinly sliced
200 g (7 oz) tinned crabmeat, drained
3 eggs
185 ml (6 fl oz/³/4 cup) pouring
(whipping) cream
90 g (3¹/4 oz/³/4 cup) grated cheddar
cheese
dill sprigs (optional)

SERVES 4–6

To make the pastry, sift the flour into a bowl. Using your fingertips, rub in the butter until the mixture resembles fine breadcrumbs. Make a well in the centre and add the iced water. Mix with a flat-bladed knife, using a cutting action, until the mixture comes together in beads. Add a little more water if the dough is too dry. Turn out onto a lightly floured work surface and gather into a ball. Divide the pastry into two portions. Cover with plastic wrap and refrigerate for 20 minutes. Preheat the oven to 190°C (375°F/Gas 5). Grease two 12 cm (4¹/2 inches) round, 4 cm (1¹/2 inches) deep flan (tart) tins.

Roll out both portions of pastry between two sheets of baking paper to fit the tins. Lift the pastry into the tins and press it well into the sides. Trim off any excess by rolling a rolling pin across the top of the tin. Refrigerate the pastry for 20 minutes. Cover the shells with baking paper, fill evenly with baking beads or uncooked rice and bake for 15 minutes, or until the pastry is dried out and golden. Remove the paper and beads and cool slightly. Reduce the oven to 180°C (350°F/Gas 4).

To make the filling, heat the butter in a small frying pan and cook the onion until just soft. Remove from the pan and drain on paper towel. Squeeze out any excess moisture from the crabmeat. Spread the onion and crabmeat over the cooled pastry, arranging the crab in the centre of the quiche. Mix the eggs, cream and cheddar in a bowl. Pour into the pastry case and, if you like, top with some dill sprigs. Bake for 40 minutes, or until lightly golden and set.

PREPARATION TIME: 40 MINUTES   COOKING TIME: 1 HOUR 5 MINUTES

ONION TART

SHORTCRUST PASTRY
150 g (5^1/$_2$ oz/1^1/$_4$ cups) plain (all-purpose) flour
90 g (3^1/$_4$ oz) chilled butter, cubed
2–3 tablespoons iced water

FILLING
25 g (1 oz) butter
7 onions, sliced
1 tablespoon dijon mustard
3 eggs, lightly beaten
125 g (4^1/$_2$ oz/^{1}/$_2$ cup) sour cream
25 g (1 oz/^{1}/$_4$ cup) freshly grated parmesan cheese

SERVES 4–6

Lightly grease a round 23 cm (9 inch) fluted flan (tart) tin. Sift the flour into a bowl. Using your fingertips, rub in the butter until the mixture resembles fine breadcrumbs. Make a well in the centre, add almost all the water and mix with a flat-bladed knife, using a cutting action, until the mixture comes together in beads. Add more water if the dough is too dry.

Gather the dough together and lift out onto a lightly floured work surface. Press together until smooth, cover with plastic wrap and refrigerate for 20 minutes. Roll out between two sheets of baking paper large enough to cover the base and side of the tart tin. Place the pastry in the tin and trim the edge. Cover with plastic wrap and refrigerate for 20 minutes.

Preheat the oven to 180°C (350°F/Gas 4). Line the pastry shell with a piece of baking paper and pour in some baking beads or uncooked rice. Bake for 10 minutes, remove the paper and beads and bake for another 10 minutes, or until lightly golden. Cool completely.

To make the filling, melt the butter in a large heavy-based frying pan. Add the onion, cover and cook over medium heat for 25 minutes. Uncover and cook for another 10 minutes, stirring often, until soft and golden. Cool.

Spread the mustard over the base of the pastry, then spread the onion over the mustard. Whisk together the eggs and sour cream and pour over the onion. Sprinkle with parmesan and bake for 35 minutes, or until set and golden.

PREPARATION TIME: 40 MINUTES +   COOKING TIME: 1 HOUR 30 MINUTES

CORN AND RED CAPSICUM QUICHES

2 sheets ready-rolled shortcrust (pie) pastry
135 g (4³/₄ oz) tinned corn kernels, drained
40 g (1¹/₂ oz/¹/₃ cup) grated cheddar cheese
¹/₂ red capsicum (pepper), seeded, membrane removed and finely chopped
2 eggs
170 ml (5¹/₂ fl oz/²/₃ cup) pouring (whipping) cream
2 teaspoons dijon mustard
dash Tabasco sauce

MAKES 24

Preheat the oven to 200°C (400°F/Gas 6). Grease two shallow 12-hole patty pans or mini muffin tins. Lay the pastry on a lightly floured work surface and cut 12 rounds from each sheet with an 8 cm (3¹/₄ inch) cutter. Line the tins with the pastry circles.

Mix the corn kernels with the cheddar and red capsicum. Beat the eggs, cream, mustard and Tabasco sauce. Divide the corn mixture evenly among the pastry cases and top with the egg mixture until almost full. Bake for 15–20 minutes, or until puffed and golden. Remove from the tins while warm and cool on wire racks.

PREPARATION TIME: 30 MINUTES   COOKING TIME: 20 MINUTES

TRIPLE CHEESE FLAN

6 sheets filo pastry
60 g (2¹/₄ oz) butter, melted

FILLING
30 g (1 oz/¹/₄ cup) grated cheddar cheese
60 g (2¹/₄ oz/¹/₂ cup) grated smoked cheese
70 g (2¹/₂ oz/¹/₂ cup) grated gruyère cheese
3 eggs, lightly beaten
125 ml (4 fl oz/¹/₂ cup) milk
185 ml (6 fl oz/³/₄ cup) pouring (whipping) cream
1 tablespoon snipped chives
2 tablespoons chopped parsley

SERVES 6

Preheat the oven to 180°C (350°F/Gas 4). Lay out the filo pastry on a flat surface and cover with a damp tea towel (dish towel) to prevent it drying out. Remove one sheet and brush it with melted butter. Place another sheet of filo over it and brush with butter. Repeat until all the sheets have been used.

Brush a 23 cm (9 inch) flan (tart) tin with melted butter or oil. Line the tin with the pastry, tucking in the edges.

To make the filling, combine all the ingredients in a bowl and mix well. Pour the filling into the tin and bake for 35 minutes, or until the filling is lightly browned and set.

PREPARATION TIME: 20 MINUTES   COOKING TIME: 35 MINUTES

TOMATO AND BOCCONCINI FLAN

185 g (6½ oz/1½ cups) plain (all-purpose) flour
100 g (3½ oz) butter, chopped
1 egg
2 tablespoons cold water
5–6 roma (plum) tomatoes
salt, to sprinkle
1 tablespoon olive oil
8 bocconcini (fresh baby mozzarella cheese) (about 220 g/7¾ oz), sliced
6 spring onions (scallions), chopped
2 tablespoons chopped rosemary

SERVES 6

Combine the flour and butter in a food processor. Process for 10 seconds, or until fine and crumbly. Combine the egg and water in a small bowl. With the motor constantly running, gradually add to the flour mixture and process until the mixture just comes together. Turn out onto a lightly floured surface and knead to form a smooth dough. Refrigerate, covered with plastic wrap, for 20 minutes.

Preheat the oven to 210°C (415°F/Gas 6–7). On a floured board, roll the pastry to fit a 23 cm (9 inch) round, loose-based flan (tart) tin. Ease the pastry into the tin and trim the edges. Cut a sheet of baking paper to cover the pastry-lined tin. Place over the pastry then spread a layer of baking beads or uncooked rice evenly over the paper. Bake for 15 minutes, then remove the paper and beads and bake for another 10 minutes, or until the pastry case is lightly golden, then cool. Reduce the oven to 180°C (350°F/Gas 4).

Cut the tomatoes in half, sprinkle with salt and drizzle with the oil. Place in an ovenproof dish, cut side up and bake for 15 minutes. Arrange the tomatoes, cut side up, over the pastry. Place the bocconcini slices and spring onion between the tomatoes. Scatter with rosemary and season. Bake for 10 minutes. Remove from the oven and cool for 10 minutes before serving.

PREPARATION TIME: 30 MINUTES +   COOKING TIME: 50 MINUTES

RATATOUILLE TARTS

PASTRY
375 g (13 oz/3 cups) plain (all-purpose) flour
175 g (6 oz) chilled butter, chopped
125 ml (4 fl oz/^{1}/$_2$ cup) iced water

FILLING
1 eggplant (aubergine) (about 500 g/ 1 lb 2 oz)
60 ml (2 fl oz/^{1}/$_4$ cup) oil
1 onion, chopped
2 garlic cloves, crushed
2 zucchini (courgettes), sliced
1 red capsicum (pepper), seeded, membrane removed and chopped
1 green capsicum (pepper), seeded, membrane removed and chopped
250 g (9 oz) cherry tomatoes, halved
1 tablespoon balsamic vinegar
125 g (4^1/$_2$ oz/1 cup) grated cheddar cheese

MAKES 12

Sift the flour into a bowl. Using your fingertips, rub in the butter until the mixture resembles fine breadcrumbs. Make a well in the centre and add the iced water. Mix with a flat-bladed knife, using a cutting action, until the dough just comes together. Add more water if the dough is too dry. Gather into a ball and divide into 12 portions.

Grease 12 loose-based fluted flan (tart) tins measuring 8 cm (3^1/$_4$ inches) across the base and 3 cm (1^1/$_4$ inches) deep. Roll each portion of dough out on a sheet of baking paper to a circle a little larger than the tins. Lift into the tins, press into the sides, then trim away any excess pastry. Refrigerate for 30 minutes. Preheat the oven to 200°C (400°F/Gas 6).

Put the tins on baking trays, prick the pastry bases all over with a fork and bake for 20–25 minutes, or until the pastry is fully cooked and lightly golden. Cool completely.

Meanwhile, to make the ratatouille filling, cut the eggplant into 2 cm (^{3}/$_4$ inch) cubes, put into a colander and sprinkle with salt. After 20 minutes, rinse, drain and pat dry with paper towel.

Heat 2 tablespoons of the oil in a large frying pan. Cook batches of eggplant for 8–10 minutes, or until browned, adding more oil if necessary. Drain on paper towel. Heat the remaining oil, add the onion and cook over medium heat for 5 minutes, or until very soft. Add the garlic and cook for 1 minute, then add the zucchini and capsicum and cook, stirring frequently, for 10 minutes, or until softened. Add the eggplant and tomatoes. Cook, stirring, for 2 minutes. Transfer to a bowl, stir in the vinegar, then cover and cool completely.

Reduce the oven to 180°C (350°F/Gas 4). Divide the mixture evenly among the pastry shells with a slotted spoon, draining off any excess liquid. Sprinkle with the cheddar and cook for 10–15 minutes, or until the cheese has melted and the tarts are warmed through.

PREPARATION TIME: 40 MINUTES +   COOKING TIME: 1 HOUR 10 MINUTES

GOAT'S CHEESE
AND APPLE TARTS

2 sheets frozen puff pastry
300 g (10^1/$_2$ oz) goat's cheese, sliced
2 cooking apples
2 tablespoons extra virgin olive oil
1 tablespoon chopped lemon thyme
sea salt flakes, to sprinkle

MAKES 24

Preheat the oven to hot 210°C (415°F/Gas 6-7). While the pastry is still frozen, cut each sheet into four squares and then each square into quarters.

Place slightly apart on a lightly greased baking tray. Set aside for a few minutes to thaw and then lay the cheese over the centre of each square of pastry, leaving a small border.

Core the unpeeled apples and slice them thinly. Interleave several slices over the pastry, making sure the cheese is covered completely. Lightly brush the apples with oil and sprinkle with lemon thyme and a little sea salt and pepper to taste.

Bake the tarts for 20-25 minutes, or until the pastry is cooked through and golden brown at the edges. The tarts are best served immediately.

PREPARATION TIME: 10 MINUTES   COOKING TIME: 25 MINUTES

NOTE: The pastry can be topped with cheese, covered and refrigerated overnight. Top with the apple just before cooking.

PUMPKIN TARTS

250 g (9 oz/2 cups) plain (all-purpose) flour
125 g (4^1/$_2$ oz) chilled butter, cubed
80 ml (2^1/$_2$ fl oz/^{1}/$_3$ cup) iced water
1.25 kg (2 lb 12 oz) pumpkin (winter squash), cut into 6 cm (2^1/$_2$ inch) pieces
125 g (4^1/$_2$ oz/^{1}/$_2$ cup) sour cream or cream cheese
sweet chilli sauce, to serve

SERVES 6

Sift the flour and a pinch of salt into a large bowl. Using your fingertips, rub in the butter until the mixture resembles fine breadcrumbs. Make a well in the centre, add the iced water and mix with a flat-bladed knife, using a cutting action, until the mixture comes together in beads. Gently gather the dough together and lift out onto a lightly floured work surface. Press into a ball, then flatten slightly into a disc, wrap in plastic wrap and refrigerate for 30 minutes.

Preheat the oven to 200°C (400°F/Gas 6). Divide the pastry into six portions, roll each one out and fit into a 10 cm (4 inch) pie dish. Trim the edge and prick the bases all over with a fork. Bake on a baking tray for 15 minutes, or until lightly golden, pressing down any pastry that puffs up. Cool, then remove from the tins.

Meanwhile, steam the pumpkin for about 15 minutes, or until tender.

Place a tablespoon of sour cream in the middle of each pastry case and pile the pumpkin pieces on top. Season and drizzle with sweet chilli sauce to taste. Return to the oven for a couple of minutes to heat through. Serve immediately.

PREPARATION TIME: 30 MINUTES +   COOKING TIME: 20 MINUTES

MUSHROOM, ASPARAGUS AND FETA TART

500 g (1 lb 2 oz) block ready-made puff
pastry, thawed
2 tablespoons oil
400 g (14 oz) sliced, small button
mushrooms
100 g (3^1/$_2$ oz) thin asparagus spears,
woody ends trimmed
2 tablespoons chopped parsley
200 g (7 oz) chopped feta cheese

SERVES 4

Divide the pastry into two and roll each portion between two sheets of baking paper. If making four tartlets, cut out two 12 cm (4^1/$_2$ inch) circles of pastry from each portion, or for two long tartlets roll each portion of pastry into a rectangle 12 x 25 cm (4^1/$_2$ x 10 inches). Preheat the oven to 200°C (400°F/Gas 6).

Heat the oil in a frying pan, add the mushroom and asparagus and stir until softened. Remove from the heat and add the parsley and feta. Stir and season. Spoon onto the pastry bases, leaving a 1.5 cm (5$/_8$ inch) border. Bake in the top half of the oven for 10–15 minutes, or until risen and brown. Serve warm or hot.

PREPARATION TIME: 30 MINUTES   COOKING TIME: 25 MINUTES

CREAMY HERB QUICHES

2 sheets ready-rolled shortcrust (pie)
pastry
2 eggs, lightly beaten
2 tablespoons milk
125 ml (4 fl oz/^{1}/$_2$ cup) pouring (whipping)
cream
2 teaspoons snipped chives
1 teaspoon chopped dill
1 teaspoon chopped thyme
1 teaspoon chopped flat-leaf (Italian)
parsley
2 tablespoons freshly grated parmesan
cheese

MAKES 24

Preheat the oven to 200°C (400°F/Gas 6). Grease two shallow 12-hole patty pans or mini muffin tins. Lay the pastry on a work surface and cut 12 rounds from each sheet with an 8 cm (3^1/$_4$ inch) cutter. Line the tins with the pastry circles.

Mix together the egg, milk, cream and herbs. Pour into the pastry cases and sprinkle with the parmesan. Bake for 15–20 minutes, or until puffed and golden. Remove from the tins while warm and cool on wire racks.

PREPARATION TIME: 20 MINUTES   COOKING TIME: 20 MINUTES

CUSTARD TARTS

PASTRY

250 g (9 oz/2 cups) plain (all-purpose) flour

60 g (2^1/$_4$ oz/^{1}/$_3$ cup) rice flour

30 g (1 oz/^{1}/$_4$ cup) icing (confectioners') sugar

120 g (4^1/$_4$ oz) chilled unsalted butter, cubed

1 egg yolk

60 ml (2 fl oz/^{1}/$_4$ cup) iced water

1 egg white, lightly beaten

CUSTARD FILLING

3 eggs

375 ml (13 fl oz/1^1/$_2$ cups) milk

55 g (2 oz/^{1}/$_4$ cup) caster (superfine) sugar

1 teaspoon natural vanilla extract

^{1}/$_2$ teaspoon freshly grated nutmeg

MAKES 12

Sift the flours and icing sugar into a large bowl. Using your fingertips, rub in the butter until the mixture resembles fine breadcrumbs. Make a well in the centre and add the egg yolk and almost all the water. Mix with a flat-bladed knife, using a cutting action, until the mixture comes together in small beads. Add more water if the dough is too dry. Gather together and roll out between two sheets of baking paper. Divide the dough into 12 equal portions and roll each portion out to fit the base and side of a 10 cm (4 inch) loose-based fluted flan (tart) tin. Line the tins with the pastry and roll the rolling pin over the tins to trim any excess pastry. Refrigerate for 20 minutes.

Preheat the oven to 180°C (350°F/Gas 4). Line each pastry-lined tin with baking paper. Fill with baking beads or uncooked rice. Place the tins on two large baking trays and bake for 10 minutes. Remove the baking paper and beads and bake for another 10 minutes, or until the pastry is lightly golden. Cool. Brush the base and side of each pastry case with beaten egg white. Reduce the oven to 150°C (300°F/Gas 2).

To make the filling, whisk the eggs and milk in a bowl to combine. Add the sugar gradually, whisking to dissolve completely. Stir in the vanilla extract. Strain, then pour into the cooled pastry cases. Sprinkle with nutmeg and bake for 25 minutes, or until the filling is just set. Serve at room temperature.

PREPARATION TIME: 30 MINUTES +   COOKING TIME: 45 MINUTES

TREACLE TART

SHORTCRUST PASTRY

150 g (5^1/$_2$ oz/1^1/$_4$ cups) plain (all-purpose) flour
90 g (3^1/$_4$ oz) chilled unsalted butter, chopped
2–3 tablespoons iced water
1 egg, lightly beaten, to glaze

FILLING

350 g (12 oz/1 cup) golden syrup or dark corn syrup
25 g (1 oz) unsalted butter
^{1}/$_2$ teaspoon ground ginger
140 g (5 oz/1^3/$_4$ cups) fresh white breadcrumbs

icing (confectioners') sugar, to dust (optional)

SERVES 4–6

To make the pastry, sift the flour into a large bowl. Using your fingertips, rub in the butter until the mixture resembles fine breadcrumbs. Add almost all the iced water and mix to a firm dough, with a flat-bladed knife, using a cutting action. Add more water if the dough is too dry. Turn onto a lightly floured work surface and gather together into a ball. Cover with plastic wrap and refrigerate for 20 minutes.

Brush a 20 cm (8 inch) diameter flan (tart) tin with melted butter or oil. Roll out the pastry large enough to fit the base and side of the tin, allowing a 4 cm (1^1/$_2$ inch) overhang. Ease the pastry into the tin and trim by running a rolling pin firmly across the top of the tin. Re-roll the trimmed pastry to a rectangle 10 x 20 cm (4 x 8 inches). Using a sharp knife or fluted pastry wheel, cut into long 1 cm (^{1}/$_2$ inch) strips. Cover the pastry-lined tin and strips with plastic wrap and refrigerate for 20 minutes. Preheat the oven to 180°C (350°F/Gas 4).

To make the filling, combine the golden syrup, butter and ginger in a small saucepan and stir over low heat until the butter melts. Stir in the breadcrumbs until combined. Pour the mixture into the pastry case. Lay half the pastry strips over the tart, starting at the centre and working outwards. Lay the remaining strips over the tart to form a lattice pattern. Brush the lattice with beaten egg. Bake for 30 minutes, or until the pastry is lightly golden. Serve warm or at room temperature. You can dust the top with icing sugar and serve with ice cream or cream.

PREPARATION TIME: 30 MINUTES +   COOKING TIME: 35 MINUTES

DATE AND MASCARPONE TART

COCONUT PASTRY

90 g (3^1/$_4$ oz/^{1}/$_2$ cup) rice flour

60 g (2^1/$_4$ oz/^{1}/$_2$ cup) plain (all-purpose) flour

100 g (3^1/$_2$ oz) chilled unsalted butter, chopped

2 tablespoons icing (confectioners') sugar

25 g (1 oz/^{1}/$_4$ cup) desiccated coconut

100 g (3^1/$_2$ oz) marzipan, grated

FILLING

8 fresh dates (about 200 g/7 oz), stoned and quartered, lengthways

2 eggs

2 teaspoons custard powder or instant vanilla pudding mix

125 g (4^1/$_2$ oz) mascarpone cheese

2 tablespoons caster (superfine) sugar

80 ml (2^1/$_2$ fl oz/^{1}/$_3$ cup) pouring (whipping) cream

2 tablespoons flaked almonds

SERVES 6–8

Preheat the oven to 180°C (350°F/Gas 4). Grease a shallow, 10 x 34 cm (4 x 13^1/$_2$ inch) fluted loose-based flan (tart) tin. Sift the flours into a large bowl. Using your fingertips, rub in the butter until the mixture resembles fine breadcrumbs, then press the mixture together gently. Stir in the icing sugar, coconut and marzipan. Turn out onto a lightly floured work surface and gather together into a ball. Flatten slightly, cover with plastic wrap and refrigerate for 15 minutes.

Roll out the pastry between two sheets of baking paper until large enough to line the tin. Ease the pastry into the tin and trim the edge. Refrigerate for 5–10 minutes. Line the pastry-lined tin with baking paper and spread a layer of baking beads or uncooked rice evenly over the paper. Place the tin on a baking tray and bake for 10 minutes. Remove the paper and beads and bake for another 5 minutes, or until just golden, then allow to cool.

Arrange the date quarters over the pastry. Whisk together the eggs, custard powder, mascarpone, caster sugar and cream until smooth. Pour the mixture over the dates, then sprinkle with the flaked almonds. Bake for 25–30 minutes, or until golden and just set, then allow to cool slightly. Serve warm.

PREPARATION TIME: 50 MINUTES +   COOKING TIME: 45 MINUTES

LEMON BRÛLÉE TARTS

310 ml (10³/₄ fl oz/1¹/₄ cups) pouring (whipping) cream
2 teaspoons grated lemon zest
4 egg yolks
2 tablespoons caster (superfine) sugar
2 teaspoons cornflour (cornstarch)
2 tablespoons lemon juice
410 g (14¹/₂ oz) block puff pastry, thawed or 2 sheets ready-rolled
80 g (2³/₄ oz/¹/₃ cup) sugar

SERVES 4

Heat the cream in a saucepan with the lemon zest until almost boiling. Allow to cool slightly. Whisk the egg yolks, sugar, cornflour and lemon juice in a bowl until thick and pale.

Add the cream gradually, whisking constantly. Strain into a clean saucepan and stir over low heat until thickened slightly — the mixture should coat the back of a wooden spoon. Pour into a heatproof bowl, cover with plastic wrap and refrigerate for several hours or overnight.

Preheat the oven to 210°C (415°F/Gas 6–7). Lightly grease four 12 cm (4¹/₂ inch) shallow loose-based flan (tart) tins. If using block pastry roll it to 25 x 48 cm (10 x 19 inches), then cut four rounds, large enough to fit the base and side of the tins. If using sheets, cut two rounds of pastry from each sheet to line the tins. Line each tin with pastry, trim the edges and prick the bases lightly with a fork. Line with baking paper and spread a layer of baking beads or uncooked rice evenly over the paper. Bake for 15 minutes, remove the paper and beads and bake for another 5 minutes, or until lightly golden. Leave to cool.

Spoon the lemon custard into each pastry shell, smooth the top, leaving a little room for the sugar layer. Cover the edges of the pastry with foil and sprinkle sugar generously over the surface of the custard in an even layer. Cook under a preheated grill (broiler) until the sugar just begins to colour. Put the tarts close to the grill so they brown quickly, but watch carefully that they do not burn. Serve immediately.

PREPARATION TIME: 40 MINUTES +   COOKING TIME: 35 MINUTES

BUTTERSCOTCH TART

SHORTCRUST PASTRY
250 g (9 oz/2 cups) plain (all-purpose) flour
125 g (4$\frac{1}{2}$ oz) chilled unsalted butter, chopped
2 tablespoons caster (superfine) sugar
1 egg yolk
1 tablespoon iced water

BUTTERSCOTCH FILLING
185 g (6$\frac{1}{2}$ oz/1 cup) soft brown sugar
40 g (1$\frac{1}{2}$ oz/$\frac{1}{3}$ cup) plain (all-purpose) flour
250 ml (9 fl oz/1 cup) milk
50 g (1$\frac{3}{4}$ oz) unsalted butter
1 teaspoon natural vanilla extract
1 egg yolk

MERINGUE
2 egg whites
2 tablespoons caster (superfine) sugar

SERVES 6–8

Preheat the oven to 180°C (350°F/Gas 4). Grease a deep 22 cm (8$\frac{1}{2}$ inch) flan (tart) tin. Sift the flour into a large bowl. Using your fingertips, rub in the butter until the mixture resembles fine breadcrumbs. Stir in the sugar, egg yolk and iced water. Mix to a soft dough with a flat-bladed knife, using a cutting action, then gather into a ball. Wrap and refrigerate for 20 minutes.

Roll the pastry between two sheets of baking paper, large enough to cover the base and side of the tin. Trim the edge and prick the pastry evenly with a fork. Refrigerate for 20 minutes. Line the pastry with baking paper and spread baking beads or uncooked rice over the paper. Bake for 35 minutes, then remove the paper and beads.

To make the filling, place the sugar and flour in a small saucepan. Make a well in the centre and gradually whisk in the milk to form a smooth paste. Add the butter and stir with a whisk over low heat for 8 minutes, or until the mixture boils and thickens. Remove from the heat, add the vanilla extract and egg yolk and whisk until smooth. Spread into the pastry case and smooth the surface.

To make the meringue, beat the egg whites until firm peaks form. Add the sugar gradually, beating until thick and glossy and all the sugar has dissolved. Spoon over the filling and swirl into peaks with a fork or flat-bladed knife. Bake for 5–10 minutes, or until the meringue is golden. Serve warm or cold.

PREPARATION TIME: 30 MINUTES +   COOKING TIME: 1 HOUR

PINE NUT TARTS

60 g (2¼ oz/½ cup) plain (all-purpose) flour
60 g (2¼ oz) unsalted butter, chopped
40 g (1½ oz/¼ cup) pine nuts
20 g (¾ oz) unsalted butter, extra, melted
175 g (6 oz/½ cup) golden syrup or dark corn syrup
2 tablespoons soft brown sugar
icing (confectioners') sugar, to dust (optional)

MAKES 24

Preheat the oven to 180°C (350°F/Gas 4). Grease two 12-hole mini muffin tins. Sift the flour into a bowl. Using your fingertips, rub in the butter until the mixture comes together. Turn onto a lightly floured surface and gather together.

Roll out on a lightly floured work surface to a thickness of 3 mm (⅛ inch). Cut out rounds with a 5 cm (2 inch) fluted cutter. Lift gently with a flat-bladed knife and line each muffin hole with pastry. Spread the pine nuts onto a flat baking tray and bake for 2–3 minutes, or until just golden. Remove from the tray and cool. Divide the nuts among the pastry cases.

Combine the melted butter, golden syrup and sugar and whisk with a fork, then pour over the pine nuts. Bake for 15 minutes, or until golden. Cool in the trays for 5 minutes before lifting out onto a wire rack to cool completely. Dust with icing sugar before serving, if desired.

PREPARATION TIME: 25 MINUTES   COOKING TIME: 20 MINUTES

PLUM TART

500 g (1 lb 2 oz) block puff pastry, thawed

TOPPING
1 tablespoon plum jam
5 large plums, very thinly sliced
1 tablespoon brandy
1 tablespoon sugar

SERVES 6

Preheat the oven to 200°C (400°F/Gas 6). Roll out the pastry on a lightly floured work surface to make an irregular rectangular shape, about 20 x 30 cm (8 x 12 inches) and 5 mm (¼ inch) thick. Place the pastry on a greased baking tray.

Heat the plum jam with 2 teaspoons water in a small saucepan over low heat until the jam is softened and spreadable. Brush the jam over the pastry base, leaving a 2 cm (¾ inch) border. Lay the plum slices along the pastry, leaving a 2 cm (¾ inch) border all around. Lightly brush the fruit with the brandy and sprinkle with the sugar. Bake for 30 minutes, or until the pastry is puffed and golden. Cut into slices and serve warm with cream or ice cream.

PREPARATION TIME: 20 MINUTES   COOKING TIME: 35 MINUTES

NOTE: This tart can also be made using four very thinly sliced large nectarines and substituting apricot jam for the plum jam.

PEAR AND ALMOND FLAN

PASTRY

150 g (5^1/$_2$ oz/1^1/$_4$ cups) plain (all-purpose) flour
90 g (3^1/$_4$ oz) chilled unsalted butter, cubed
55 g (2 oz/^{1}/$_4$ cup) caster (superfine) sugar
2 egg yolks, lightly beaten

FILLING

165 g (5^3/$_4$ oz) unsalted butter, softened
150 g (5^1/$_2$ oz/^{2}/$_3$ cup) caster (superfine) sugar
3 eggs
125 g (4^1/$_2$ oz/1^1/$_4$ cups) ground almonds
1^1/$_2$ tablespoons plain (all-purpose) flour
2 very ripe pears

SERVES 8

Lightly grease a shallow 24 cm (9^1/$_2$ inch) round, loose-based, fluted flan (tart) tin.

To make the pastry, sift the flour into a bowl. Using your fingertips, rub in the butter until the mixture resembles fine breadcrumbs. Stir in the caster sugar and mix together. Make a well in the centre, add the egg yolks and mix with a flat-bladed knife, using a cutting action, until the mixture comes together in beads. Turn out onto a lightly floured work surface and gather into a ball. Wrap in plastic wrap and refrigerate for 30 minutes.

Preheat the oven to 180°C (350°F/Gas 4). Roll out the pastry between two sheets of baking paper until large enough to line the base and side of the tin. Line the tin with the pastry and trim the edge. Sparsely prick the base with a fork. Line the base with baking paper, pour in some baking beads or uncooked rice and bake for 10 minutes. Remove the paper and beads and bake for another 10 minutes. Cool.

To make the filling, beat the butter and sugar in a bowl using electric beaters for 30 seconds (don't cream the mixture). Add the eggs one at a time, beating after each addition. Fold in the ground almonds and flour and spread the filling smoothly over the cooled pastry base.

Peel the pears, halve lengthways and remove the cores. Cut crossways into 3 mm (^{1}/$_8$ inch) slices. Separate the slices slightly, then place the slices on top of the tart to form a cross. Bake for about 50 minutes, or until the filling has set (the middle may still be a little soft). Cool in the tin, then refrigerate for at least 2 hours before serving. Can be dusted with icing sugar.

PREPARATION TIME: 15 MINUTES +   COOKING TIME: 1 HOUR 10 MINUTES

LATTICE MINCEMEAT TARTS

PASTRY
60 g (2$^{1}/_{4}$ oz/$^{1}/_{2}$ cup) self-raising flour
185 g (6$^{1}/_{2}$ oz/1$^{1}/_{2}$ cups) plain (all-purpose) flour
125 g (4$^{1}/_{2}$ oz) chilled unsalted butter, chopped
2 tablespoons caster (superfine) sugar
2–3 tablespoons iced water

MINCEMEAT
35 g (1$^{1}/_{4}$ oz/$^{1}/_{4}$ cup) currants
40 g (1$^{1}/_{2}$ oz/$^{1}/_{3}$ cup) sultanas (golden raisins)
2 tablespoons mixed peel (mixed candied citrus peel)
30 g (1 oz/$^{1}/_{4}$ cup) slivered almonds
50 g (1$^{3}/_{4}$ oz/$^{1}/_{4}$ cup) soft brown sugar
$^{1}/_{4}$ teaspoon freshly grated nutmeg
$^{1}/_{4}$ teaspoon ground cinnamon
1 apple, grated
1 teaspoon grated orange zest
1 teaspoon grated lemon zest
100 g (3$^{1}/_{2}$ oz) pitted fresh cherries
100 g (3$^{1}/_{2}$ oz) white grapes, halved
1 tablespoon whisky

1 egg, lightly beaten, to glaze
icing (confectioners') sugar, to dust

SERVES 6

Preheat the oven to 200°C (400°F/Gas 6). Brush six 8 cm (3$^{1}/_{4}$ inch) fluted loose-based 3 cm (1$^{1}/_{4}$ inch) deep flan (tart) tins with oil or melted butter.

To make the pastry, sift the flours into a bowl. Using your fingertips, rub in the butter until the mixture resembles fine breadcrumbs. Stir in the sugar and mix in the iced water with a flat-bladed knife, using a cutting action. Turn onto a lightly floured work surface and gather together. Wrap in plastic wrap and refrigerate for 15 minutes.

Set aside one-quarter of the dough. Divide the remaining dough into six. Roll each portion out and line the base and side of the tins. Refrigerate for 10 minutes. Line the pastry cases with crumpled baking paper and fill with baking beads or uncooked rice. Bake for 10 minutes, remove the paper and beads and bake for another 10 minutes. Cool. Reduce the oven to 180°C (350°F/Gas 4).

Mix together all the mincemeat ingredients. Divide the mixture evenly among the pastry cases.

Roll out the remaining pastry on a lightly floured surface to 3 mm ($^{1}/_{8}$ inch) thick. Using a lattice pastry cutter (see Note), run it along the length of the pastry. Gently pull the lattice open. Using a 10 cm (4 inch) cutter, cut out six rounds. Brush the tart edges with beaten egg, place the pastry lattice rounds on top and press gently to seal. Brush with beaten egg and bake for 45 minutes, or until golden brown. Leave in the tin for 5 minutes, then carefully remove and cool on a rack. Dust with icing sugar before serving.

PREPARATION TIME: 40 MINUTES   COOKING TIME: 1 HOUR 10 MINUTES

NOTE: Special lattice cutters are available from speciality kitchenware stores. If you cannot obtain these, simply cut straight lines instead.

RASPBERRY SHORTCAKE

PASTRY

125 g (4$\frac{1}{2}$ oz/1 cup) plain
(all-purpose) flour
40 g (1$\frac{1}{2}$ oz/$\frac{1}{3}$ cup) icing
(confectioners') sugar
90 g (3$\frac{1}{4}$ oz) chilled unsalted
butter, chopped
1 egg yolk
$\frac{1}{2}$ teaspoon natural vanilla extract
$\frac{1}{2}$–1 tablespoon iced water

TOPPING

750 g (1 lb 10 oz/6 cups) fresh raspberries
30 g (1 oz/$\frac{1}{4}$ cup) icing (confectioners')
sugar
110 g (3$\frac{3}{4}$ oz/$\frac{1}{3}$ cup) redcurrant jelly

pouring (whipping) cream, to serve

SERVES 6–8

To make the pastry, sift the flour and icing sugar into a large bowl. Using your fingertips, rub in the butter until the mixture resembles fine breadcrumbs. Add the egg yolk, vanilla extract and enough of the iced water to make the ingredients come together, then mix to a dough with a flat-bladed knife, using a cutting action. Turn out onto a lightly floured work surface and gather together into a ball. Flatten slightly, wrap in plastic wrap and refrigerate for 30 minutes.

Preheat the oven to 180°C (350°F/Gas 4). Roll out the pastry to fit a fluted 10 x 34 cm (4 x 13$\frac{1}{2}$ inch) loose-based flan (tart) tin and trim the edge. Prick all over with a fork and refrigerate for 20 minutes. Line the pastry with baking paper and spread a layer of baking beads or uncooked rice evenly over the paper. Bake for 15–20 minutes, or until golden. Remove the paper and beads and bake for another 15 minutes. Cool on a wire rack.

To make the topping, set aside 500 g (1 lb 2 oz/4 cups) of the best raspberries and mash the rest with the icing sugar. Spread the mashed raspberries over the shortcake just before serving.

Cover with the whole raspberries. Heat the redcurrant jelly in a small saucepan until melted and smooth. Use a soft pastry brush to coat the raspberries heavily with warm glaze. Cut into slices and serve with cream.

PREPARATION TIME: 30 MINUTES + COOKING TIME: 35 MINUTES

NOTE: Strawberry shortcake is a classic American dish. It is usually made as a round of shortcake which is split, then filled or topped with fresh strawberries.

LINZERTORTE

100 g (3$\frac{1}{2}$ oz/$\frac{2}{3}$ cup) blanched almonds

185 g (6$\frac{1}{2}$ oz/1$\frac{1}{2}$ cups) plain (all-purpose) flour

$\frac{1}{2}$ teaspoon ground cinnamon

90 g (3$\frac{1}{4}$ oz) chilled unsalted butter, cubed

55 g (2 oz/$\frac{1}{4}$ cup) caster (superfine) sugar

1 egg yolk

2–3 tablespoons lemon juice or water

320 g (11$\frac{1}{4}$ oz/1 cup) raspberry jam

1 egg yolk, extra, to glaze

80 g (2$\frac{3}{4}$ oz/$\frac{1}{4}$ cup) apricot jam

SERVES 6–8

Grind the almonds in a food processor until they are the consistency of medium coarse meal. Put the flour and cinnamon in a bowl. Using your fingertips, rub in the butter until the mixture resembles fine breadcrumbs. Stir in the caster sugar and almonds. Make a well in the centre and add the egg yolk and lemon juice. Mix with a flat-bladed knife, using a cutting action, until the mixture comes together in beads. Turn onto a lightly floured work surface and knead briefly until smooth. Wrap in plastic wrap and refrigerate for at least 20 minutes to firm.

Roll two-thirds of the pastry out between two sheets of baking paper into a circle to fit a 20 cm (8 inch) round, loose-based, fluted flan (tart) tin. Press into the tin and trim away any excess pastry. Spread the raspberry jam over the base.

Roll out the remaining pastry, including any scraps, to a thickness of 3 mm ($\frac{1}{8}$ inch). Cut it into 2 cm ($\frac{3}{4}$ inch) strips with a fluted cutter. Lay half the strips on a sheet of baking paper, leaving a 1 cm ($\frac{1}{2}$ inch) gap between each strip. Interweave the remaining strips to form a lattice pattern. Invert the lattice on top of the tart, remove the paper and trim the edge with a sharp knife. Cover with plastic wrap and refrigerate for 20 minutes.

Preheat the oven to 180°C (350°F/Gas 4). Place a baking tray in the oven to heat. Combine the extra egg yolk with 1 teaspoon water and brush over the tart. Place the tin on the heated tray and bake for 25–30 minutes, or until the pastry is golden brown.

Meanwhile, heat the apricot jam with 1 tablespoon of water, then strain the jam and brush over the tart while hot. Leave to cool in the tin, then remove and cut into wedges.

PREPARATION TIME: 30 MINUTES +   COOKING TIME: 30 MINUTES

NOTE: Fluted cutters or special lattice cutters are available from speciality kitchenware stores. If you cannot obtain these, simply cut straight lines instead.

TARTE AU CITRON

PASTRY

125 g (4$\frac{1}{2}$ oz/1 cup) plain
(all-purpose) flour

80 g (2$\frac{3}{4}$ oz) unsalted butter, softened

1 egg yolk

2 tablespoons icing (confectioners')
sugar, sifted

3 eggs

2 egg yolks

175 g (6 oz/$\frac{3}{4}$ cup) caster
(superfine) sugar

125 ml (4 fl oz/$\frac{1}{2}$ cup) pouring
(whipping) cream

185 ml (6 fl oz/$\frac{3}{4}$ cup) lemon juice

1$\frac{1}{2}$ tablespoons finely grated lemon zest

2 small lemons

140 g (5 oz/$\frac{2}{3}$ cup) sugar

SERVES 6–8

To make the pastry, sift the flour and a pinch of salt into a large bowl. Make a well in the centre and add the butter, egg yolk and icing sugar. Work together the butter, yolk and sugar with your fingertips, then slowly incorporate the flour. Bring together into a ball — you may need to add a few drops of cold water. Flatten the ball slightly, cover with plastic wrap and refrigerate for 20 minutes.

Preheat the oven to 200°C (400°F/Gas 6). Lightly grease a shallow loose-based flan (tart) tin, about 2 cm ($\frac{3}{4}$ inch) deep and 21 cm (8$\frac{1}{4}$ inches) across the base.

Roll out the pastry between two sheets of baking paper until it is 3 mm ($\frac{1}{8}$ inch) thick, to fit the base and side of the tin. Trim the edge. Refrigerate for 10 minutes. Line the pastry with baking paper, fill with baking beads or uncooked rice and bake for 10 minutes. Remove the paper and beads and bake for another 6–8 minutes, or until the pastry looks dry all over. Cool the pastry and reduce the oven to 150°C (300°F/Gas 2).

Whisk the eggs, egg yolks and sugar together, add the cream and lemon juice and mix well. Strain and then add the lemon zest. Place the flan tin on a baking sheet on the middle shelf of the oven and carefully pour in the filling right up to the top. Bake for 40 minutes, or until it is just set — it should wobble in the middle when the tin is firmly tapped. Cool the tart before removing from its tin.

Meanwhile, wash and scrub the lemons well. Slice very thinly (2 mm/$\frac{1}{16}$ inch thick). Combine the sugar and 200 ml (7 fl oz) water in a small frying pan and stir over low heat until the sugar has dissolved. Add the lemon slices and simmer over low heat for 40 minutes, or until the peel is very tender and the pith looks transparent. Lift out of the syrup and drain on baking paper. If serving the tart immediately, cover the surface with the lemon slices. If not, keep the slices covered and decorate the tart when ready to serve. Serve warm or chilled, with a little cream.

PREPARATION TIME: 1 HOUR +   COOKING TIME: 1 HOUR 40 MINUTES

PORTUGUESE CUSTARD TARTS

150 g (5¹/₂ oz/1¹/₄ cups) plain (all-purpose) flour

25 g (1 oz) Copha (white vegetable shortening), chopped and softened

30 g (1 oz) unsalted butter, chopped and softened

220 g (7³/₄ oz/1 cup) sugar

500 ml (17 fl oz/2 cups) milk

30 g (1 oz/¹/₄ cup) cornflour (cornstarch)

1 tablespoon custard powder or instant vanilla pudding mix

4 egg yolks

1 teaspoon natural vanilla extract

MAKES 12

Sift the flour into a large bowl and add about 185 ml (6 fl oz/³/₄ cup) water, or enough to form a soft dough. Gather the dough into a ball, then roll out on baking paper to form a 24 x 30 cm (9¹/₂ x 12 inch) rectangle. Spread the Copha over the surface. Roll up from the short edge to form a log. Roll the dough out into a rectangle again and spread with the butter. Roll up again into a roll and slice into 12 even pieces. Working from the centre outwards, use your fingertips to press each round out to a circle large enough to cover the base and side of twelve 80 ml (2¹/₂ fl oz/¹/₃ cup) muffin holes. Press into the holes and refrigerate while preparing the filling.

Put the sugar and 80 ml (2¹/₂ fl oz/¹/₃ cup) water in a saucepan and stir over low heat until the sugar dissolves. Stir a little of the milk with the cornflour and custard powder in a small bowl to form a smooth paste. Add to the pan with the remaining milk, egg yolks and vanilla. Stir over low heat until the mixture thickens. Transfer to a bowl, cover and cool.

Preheat the oven to 220°C (425°F/Gas 7). Divide the filling among the pastry bases and bake for 25–30 minutes, or until the custard is set and the tops have browned. Cool in the tins, then transfer to a wire rack.

PREPARATION TIME: 40 MINUTES   COOKING TIME: 40 MINUTES

BANANA AND BLUEBERRY TART

125 g (4¹/₂ oz/1 cup) plain (all-purpose) flour

60 g (2¹/₄ oz/¹/₂ cup) self-raising flour

1 teaspoon cinnamon

1 teaspoon ground ginger

40 g (1¹/₂ oz) unsalted butter, chopped

100 g (3¹/₂ oz/¹/₂ cup) soft brown sugar

125 ml (4 fl oz/¹/₂ cup) buttermilk

200 g (7 oz) blueberries

2 bananas

2 teaspoons lemon juice

1 tablespoon raw (demerara) sugar

SERVES 6

Preheat the oven to 200°C (400°F/Gas 6). Spray a baking tray or pizza tray lightly with oil. Sift the flours and spices into a bowl. Add the butter and brown sugar, and rub in with your fingertips until the butter is combined well with the flour. Make a well in the centre and add enough buttermilk to mix to a soft dough. Cover with plastic wrap and refrigerate for 30 minutes.

Roll the dough out on a lightly floured surface to a 23 cm (9 inch) round. Place on the tray and roll the edge to form a lip to hold in the fruit.

Spread the blueberries over the dough, keeping them within the lip. Slice the bananas and toss the slices in the lemon juice. Arrange the banana evenly over the top of the blueberries, then sprinkle with the raw sugar and bake for 25 minutes, or until the base is browned. Serve immediately.

PREPARATION TIME: 30 MINUTES   COOKING TIME: 25 MINUTES

LEMON ALMOND TART

LEMON PASTRY

250 g (9 oz/2 cups) plain (all-purpose) flour, sifted

55 g (2 oz/¼ cup) caster (superfine) sugar

125 g (4½ oz) chilled unsalted butter, softened

1 teaspoon finely grated lemon zest

2 egg yolks

FILLING

350 g (12 oz) ricotta cheese, sieved

80 g (2¾ oz/⅓ cup) caster (superfine) sugar

3 eggs, well beaten

1 tablespoon finely grated lemon zest

80 g (2¾ oz/½ cup) blanched almonds, finely chopped

30 g (1 oz/⅓ cup) flaked almonds

icing (confectioners') sugar, to dust (optional)

SERVES 6–8

Combine the flour, sugar and a pinch of salt in a large bowl. Make a well in the centre and add the butter, lemon zest and egg yolks. Work the flour into the centre with the fingertips of one hand until a smooth dough forms (add a little more flour if necessary). Cover in plastic wrap, flatten slightly, then refrigerate for 20 minutes.

To make the filling, beat the ricotta and sugar together using electric beaters. Add the eggs gradually, beating well after each addition. Add the lemon zest, beating briefly to combine, and then stir in the chopped almonds.

Preheat the oven to 180°C (350°F/Gas 4). Brush a 20 cm (8 inch) fluted loose-based flan (tart) tin with melted butter. Roll out the pastry on a lightly floured work surface large enough to line the tin. Line the tin with the pastry, trimming away the excess. Pour in the filling and smooth the top. Sprinkle with the flaked almonds and bake for 55–60 minutes, or until lightly golden and set.

Allow to cool. Lightly dust with icing sugar, if desired, and serve at room temperature or chilled.

PREPARATION TIME: 40 MINUTES +   COOKING TIME: 1 HOUR

SUMMER BERRY TART

PASTRY

125 g (4½ oz/1 cup) plain (all-purpose) flour
90 g (3¼ oz) chilled unsalted butter, cubed
2 tablespoons icing (confectioners') sugar
1–2 tablespoons iced water

FILLING

3 egg yolks
2 tablespoons caster (superfine) sugar
2 tablespoons cornflour (cornstarch)
250 ml (9 fl oz/1 cup) milk
1 teaspoon natural vanilla extract
250 g (9 oz/1⅔ cups) strawberries, halved
125 g (4½ oz) blueberries
125 g (4½ oz/1 cup) raspberries
1–2 tablespoons baby apple gel

SERVES 4–6

Preheat the oven to 180°C (350°F/Gas 4). Lightly grease a 20 cm (8 inch) round, loose-based, fluted flan (tart) tin.

To make the pastry, sift the flour into a bowl. Using your fingertips, rub in the butter until the mixture resembles fine breadcrumbs. Mix in the sugar. Make a well in the centre and add almost all the water. Mix with a flat-bladed knife, using a cutting action, until the mixture comes together in beads. Add more water if the dough is too dry.

Roll out the pastry between two sheets of baking paper to fit the base and side of the tin. Line the tin with the pastry and trim away any excess. Refrigerate for 20 minutes. Line the tin with baking paper and spread a layer of baking beads or uncooked rice evenly over the paper. Bake for 15 minutes, remove the paper and beads and bake for another 15 minutes, or until golden.

To make the filling, put the egg yolks, sugar and cornflour in a bowl and whisk until pale. Heat the milk in a small saucepan until almost boiling, then remove from the heat and add gradually to the egg mixture, beating constantly. Strain into the pan. Stir constantly over low heat for 3 minutes, or until the mixture boils and thickens. Remove from the heat and add the vanilla extract. Transfer to a bowl, cover with plastic wrap and set aside to cool.

Spread the filling in the pastry shell and top with the berries. Heat the apple gel in a heatproof bowl in a saucepan of simmering water, or in the microwave, until it liquefies. Brush over the fruit with a pastry brush. Allow to set before cutting.

PREPARATION TIME: 35 MINUTES +   COOKING TIME: 35 MINUTES

APPLE TARTE TATIN

210 g (7$\frac{1}{2}$ oz/1$\frac{2}{3}$ cups) plain (all-purpose) flour
125 g (4$\frac{1}{2}$ oz) chilled unsalted butter, cubed
2 tablespoons caster (superfine) sugar
1 egg, lightly beaten
2 drops natural vanilla extract
8 granny smith apples
110 g (3$\frac{3}{4}$ oz/$\frac{1}{2}$ cup) sugar
40 g (1$\frac{1}{2}$ oz) unsalted butter, extra, chopped

SERVES 6

Sift the flour into a bowl. Using your fingertips, rub in the butter until the mixture resembles fine breadcrumbs. Stir in the caster sugar, then make a well in the centre. Add the egg and vanilla extract and mix with a flat-bladed knife, using a cutting action, until the mixture comes together in beads. Gather the dough together, then turn out onto a lightly floured work surface and shape into a disc. Wrap in plastic wrap and refrigerate for at least 30 minutes, to firm.

Peel and core the apples and cut each into eight slices. Put the sugar and 1 tablespoon water in a heavy-based 25 cm (10 inch) frying pan that has a metal or removable handle, so that it can safely be placed in the oven. Stir over low heat for 1 minute, or until the sugar has dissolved. Increase the heat to medium and cook for 4-5 minutes, or until the caramel turns golden. Add the extra butter and stir to incorporate. Remove from the heat.

Place the apple slices in neat circles to cover the base of the frying pan. Return the pan to low heat and cook for 10-12 minutes, or until the apples are tender and caramelized. Remove the pan from the heat and leave to cool for 10 minutes.

Preheat the oven to 220°C (425°F/Gas 7). Roll the pastry out on a lightly floured surface to a circle 1 cm ($\frac{1}{2}$ inch) larger than the frying pan. Place the pastry over the apples to cover them completely, tucking it down firmly at the edges. Bake for 30-35 minutes, or until the pastry is cooked. Leave for 15 minutes before turning out onto a plate. Serve warm or cold with cream or ice cream.

PREPARATION TIME: 30 MINUTES +   COOKING TIME: 55 MINUTES

NOTE: Special high-sided tatin tins are available from speciality kitchenware shops.

FRUIT TART

SHORTCRUST PASTRY

150 g (5^1/$_2$ oz/1^1/$_4$ cups) plain (all-purpose) flour
2 tablespoons caster (superfine) sugar
90 g (3^1/$_4$ oz) chilled unsalted butter, chopped
1 egg yolk
1 tablespoon iced water

FILLING

250 ml (9 fl oz/1 cup) milk
3 egg yolks
55 g (2 oz/^{1}/$_4$ cup) caster (superfine) sugar
2 tablespoons plain (all-purpose) flour
1 teaspoon natural vanilla extract
strawberries, kiwi fruit and blueberries, to decorate
apricot jam, to glaze

SERVES 6

Sift the flour into a bowl and stir in the sugar. Using your fingertips, rub in the butter until the mixture resembles fine breadcrumbs. Make a well in the centre and add the egg yolk and iced water. Mix to a dough with a flat-bladed knife, using a cutting action. Turn out onto a lightly floured work surface and gather together into a ball. Press together gently until smooth, and then roll out to fit a 10 x 34 cm (4 x 13^1/$_2$ inch) loose-based fluted flan (tart) tin. Line the tin with pastry and trim away any excess. Wrap in plastic wrap and refrigerate for 20 minutes. Preheat the oven to 190°C (375°F/Gas 5).

Line the pastry-lined tin with baking paper and spread a layer of baking beads or uncooked rice evenly over the paper. Bake for 15 minutes, remove the paper and beads and bake for another 20 minutes, or until cooked on the base and golden brown around the edge. Set aside to cool completely.

To make the filling, put the milk into a small saucepan and bring to the boil. Set aside while quickly whisking the egg yolks and sugar together in a bowl, until light and creamy. Whisk in the flour. Pour the hot milk slowly onto the egg mixture, whisking constantly. Wash out the pan, return the milk mixture to the pan and bring to the boil over medium heat, stirring with a wire whisk. Boil for 2 minutes, stirring occasionally. Transfer to a bowl, stir in the vanilla extract, and leave to cool, stirring frequently to avoid a skin forming. When cooled to room temperature, cover the surface with plastic wrap and refrigerate until cold.

Cut the strawberries in half and peel and slice the kiwi fruit. Spoon the cold custard into the cold pastry shell, then arrange all the fruit over the custard, pressing in slightly. Heat the jam in the microwave or in a small saucepan until liquid, sieve to remove any lumps, then, using a pastry brush, glaze the fruit with the jam. Serve the tart on the same day, at room temperature. If it is to be left for a while on a hot day, refrigerate it.

PREPARATION TIME: 40 MINUTES +   COOKING TIME: 40 MINUTES

NOTE: If you don't have a rectangular tin, this tart may be made in a 23 cm (9 inch) round flan tin. You can use different fruits to top the tart, according to taste and season.

PASSIONFRUIT TART

90 g (3$\frac{1}{4}$ oz/$\frac{3}{4}$ cup) plain (all-purpose) flour

2 tablespoons icing (confectioners') sugar

2 tablespoons custard powder or instant vanilla pudding mix

30 g (1 oz) unsalted butter

60 ml (2 fl oz/$\frac{1}{4}$ cup) light evaporated milk

icing (confectioners') sugar, extra, to dust

FILLING

pulp from about 8 passionfruit

125 g (4$\frac{1}{2}$ oz/$\frac{1}{2}$ cup) ricotta cheese

1 teaspoon natural vanilla extract

30 g (1 oz/$\frac{1}{4}$ cup) icing (confectioners') sugar

2 eggs, lightly beaten

185 ml (6 fl oz/$\frac{3}{4}$ cup) light evaporated milk

SERVES 8

Preheat the oven to 200°C (400°F/Gas 6). Lightly spray a 23 cm (9 inch) loose-based flan (tart) tin with oil spray. Sift the flour, icing sugar and custard powder into a bowl. Using your fingertips, rub in the butter until the mixture resembles fine breadcrumbs. Add almost all the milk. Mix with a flat-bladed knife, using a cutting action, until the mixture forms a soft dough. Add more milk if the dough is too dry. Bring together on a lightly floured work surface until just smooth. Form into a ball, wrap in plastic wrap and refrigerate for 15 minutes.

Roll the pastry out on a lightly floured surface, large enough to fit the tin, then refrigerate for 15 minutes. Cover with baking paper and fill with baking beads or uncooked rice. Bake for 10 minutes, remove the paper and beads and bake for another 5–8 minutes, or until golden. Cool. Reduce the oven to 160°C (315°F/Gas 2–3).

Strain the passionfruit pulp to remove the seeds, reserving 2 teaspoons of seeds. Beat the ricotta with the vanilla extract and icing sugar until smooth. Add the eggs and passionfruit pulp, reserved seeds and milk, then beat well. Put the tin on a baking tray and gently pour in the mixture. Bake for 40 minutes, or until set. Cool in the tin. Dust the edges with icing sugar just before serving.

PREPARATION TIME: 30 MINUTES + COOKING TIME: 1 HOUR

BANANA TART

FLAKY PASTRY

220 g (7³/4 oz/1³/4 cups) plain
(all-purpose) flour
60 g (2¹/4 oz) unsalted butter
150 ml (5 fl oz) iced water
100 g (3¹/2 oz) unsalted butter, extra,
chilled

zest and juice of 2 oranges
80 g (2³/4 oz/¹/3 cup) soft brown sugar
¹/4 teaspoon cardamom seeds
1 tablespoon rum
3-4 ripe bananas

SERVES 6

To make the pastry, sift the flour into a bowl with a pinch of salt. Using your fingertips, rub in the butter until the mixture resembles fine breadcrumbs. Add enough of the iced water, mixing with a flat-bladed knife and using a cutting action, to make a dough-like consistency. Turn onto a lightly floured work surface and knead until just smooth.

Roll into a rectangle 10 x 30 cm (4 x 12 inches), cut one-third of the extra chilled butter into cubes and dot all over the top two-thirds of the pastry, leaving a little room around the edge. Fold the bottom third of the pastry up and the top third down and press the edges down to seal. Now turn the pastry to your left, so the hinge is on your right, and roll and fold as before. Refrigerate for 20 minutes, then with the hinge to your right, roll it out again, cover the top two-thirds of the pastry with another third of the butter and roll and fold. Repeat, using the rest of the butter and then roll and fold once more without adding any butter.

Roll the pastry out on a lightly floured work surface into a rectangle 25 x 30 cm (10 x 12 inches), cut a 2 cm (³/4 inch) strip off each side and use this to make a frame on the pastry by brushing the edges of the pastry with water and sticking the strips onto it. Trim off any excess and put the tart base on a baking tray lined with baking paper, cover with plastic wrap and refrigerate until required.

Combine the orange zest, juice, brown sugar and cardamom seeds in a small saucepan, bring to the boil, simmer for 5 minutes, then remove from the heat and add the rum. Set aside to cool. Preheat the oven to 220°C (425°F/Gas 7).

Slice the bananas in half lengthways, arrange on the tart in an even layer, cut side up, and brush with a little syrup. Bake on the top shelf of the oven for 20–30 minutes, making sure the pastry does not overbrown. Brush with syrup and serve.

PREPARATION TIME: 40 MINUTES +   COOKING TIME: 35 MINUTES

TURNOVERS AND OTHER PASTRIES

VEGETABLE STRUDEL

12 English spinach leaves
2 tablespoons olive oil
1 onion, finely sliced
1 red capsicum (pepper), seeded, membrane removed and cut into strips
1 green capsicum (pepper), seeded, membrane removed and cut into strips
2 zucchinis (courgettes), sliced
2 slender eggplants (aubergines), sliced
6 sheets filo pastry
40 g (1½ oz) butter, melted
20 g (¾ oz) finely sliced basil leaves
60 g (2¼ oz/½ cup) grated cheddar cheese
2 tablespoons sesame seeds

SERVES 4–6

Preheat the oven to 210°C (415°F/Gas 6-7). Brush an oven tray with melted butter or oil. Wash the spinach leaves thoroughly and steam or microwave them until they are just softened. Squeeze out any excess moisture and spread the leaves out to dry.

Heat the oil in a frying pan, add the onion and cook over medium heat for 3 minutes. Add the capsicum, zucchini and eggplant and cook, stirring, for 5 minutes, or until the vegetables have softened. Season and then set aside to cool.

Brush one sheet of filo pastry with melted butter and top with a second sheet. Repeat with the remaining pastry, brushing with butter between each layer. Place the spinach, cooled vegetable mixture, basil and cheese along one long side of the pastry, about 5 cm (2 inches) in from the edge. Fold the sides over the filling, fold the short end over and roll up tightly.

Place the strudel, seam side down, on the prepared tray. Brush with the remaining melted butter and sprinkle with the sesame seeds. Bake for 25 minutes, or until golden brown and crisp.

PREPARATION TIME: 30 MINUTES   COOKING TIME: 35 MINUTES

NOTE: This dish is best made just before serving. Serve sliced as a first course, or with a green salad as a main meal.

EMPANADAS

60 ml (2 fl oz/¼ cup) olive oil
250 g (9 oz) onions, finely diced
4 spring onions (scallions), thinly sliced
3 garlic cloves, crushed
200 g (7 oz) minced (ground) beef
2 teaspoons ground cumin
2 teaspoons dried oregano
250 g (9 oz) potatoes, cut into small cubes
500 g (1 lb 2 oz) block ready-made puff pastry, thawed
100 g (3½ oz) black olives, pitted and quartered
2 hard-boiled eggs, finely chopped
1 egg, separated
pinch paprika
pinch sugar

SERVES 8

Heat 1 tablespoon of the oil in a frying pan, add the onion and spring onion and stir over low heat for 5 minutes. Stir in the garlic and cook for 3 minutes. Remove from the pan.

Heat another tablespoon of oil in the pan, add the beef and stir over medium heat until browned, breaking up any lumps with a fork. Return the onion mixture and stir well. Add the cumin, oregano and 1 teaspoon each of salt and pepper, and stir for another 2 minutes. Transfer to a bowl and allow to cool. Wipe out the pan.

Heat the remaining oil in the pan, add the potato and stir over high heat for 1 minute. Reduce the heat to low and stir for 5 minutes, or until tender. Transfer to a plate to cool. Gently mix the potato into the beef mixture. Preheat the oven to 200°C (400°F/Gas 6). Grease two baking trays.

Divide the pastry into two portions and roll out each piece on a lightly floured surface until 3 mm (⅛ inch) thick. Cut out rounds, using a 10 cm (4 inch) cutter.

Spoon the beef mixture onto one half of each pastry round, leaving a border all around. Place a few olive pieces and some chopped egg on top. Brush the pastry border with egg white. Fold each pastry over to make a half-moon shape, pressing firmly to seal. Press the edges with a floured fork, then transfer to the trays. Mix the egg yolk, paprika and sugar and brush over the empanadas. Bake for 15 minutes, or until golden.

PREPARATION TIME: 1 HOUR 10 MINUTES   COOKING TIME: 45 MINUTES

CHICKEN AND BACON GOUGÈRE

60 g (2¼ oz) butter
1–2 garlic cloves, crushed
1 red onion, chopped
3 bacon slices, chopped
30 g (1 oz/¼ cup) plain (all-purpose) flour
375 ml (13 fl oz/1½ cups) milk
125 ml (4 fl oz/½ cup) pouring (whipping) cream
2 teaspoons wholegrain mustard
250 g (9 oz) cooked chicken, chopped
30 g (1 oz) chopped parsley

CHOUX PASTRY
60 g (2¼ oz/½ cup) plain (all-purpose) flour
60 g (2¼ oz) chilled butter, cubed
2 eggs, lightly beaten
35 g (1¼ oz/⅓ cup) freshly grated parmesan cheese

SERVES 6

Melt the butter in a frying pan, add the garlic, onion and bacon and cook for 5–7 minutes, stirring occasionally, or until cooked but not brown. Stir in the flour and cook for 1 minute. Gradually add the milk and stir until thickened. Simmer for 2 minutes, then add the cream and mustard. Remove from the heat and fold in the chicken and parsley. Season with pepper.

To make the choux pastry, sift the flour onto a piece of baking paper. Put the butter in a large saucepan with 125 ml (4 fl oz/½ cup) water and stir over medium heat until the mixture comes to the boil. Remove from the heat, add the flour in one go and quickly beat it into the water with a wooden spoon. Return to the heat and continue beating until the mixture forms a ball and leaves the side of the pan. Transfer to a large clean bowl and cool slightly. Beat the mixture to release any more heat. Gradually add the beaten egg, about 3 teaspoons at a time. Beat well after each addition until all the egg has been added and the mixture is thick and glossy — a wooden spoon should stand up in it. If it is too runny, the egg has been added too quickly. If so, beat for several minutes more, or until thickened. Add the parmesan.

Preheat the oven to 210°C (415°F/Gas 6–7). Grease a deep 23 cm (9 inch) ovenproof dish, pour in the filling and spoon heaped tablespoons of choux around the outside. Bake for 10 minutes, then reduce the oven to 180°C (350°F/Gas 4). Bake for 20 minutes, or until the choux is puffed and golden. Sprinkle with a little more grated parmesan if desired.

PREPARATION TIME: 40 MINUTES   COOKING TIME: 50 MINUTES

HAM AND OLIVE EMPANADILLAS

2 hard-boiled eggs, roughly chopped
40 g (1½ oz) stuffed green olives, chopped
100 g (3½ oz) ham, finely chopped
30 g (1 oz) cheddar cheese, grated
3 sheets ready-rolled puff pastry, thawed
1 egg yolk, lightly beaten

MAKES ABOUT 15

Preheat the oven to 220°C (425°F/Gas 7). Lightly grease two baking trays. Combine the egg with the olives, ham and cheddar in a bowl.

Cut the puff pastry sheets into 10 cm (4 inch) rounds (about five rounds from each sheet.) Spoon a tablespoon of the egg mixture into the centre of each round, fold over the pastry to enclose the filling and crimp the edges to seal.

Place the pastries on the trays 2 cm (¾ inch) apart. Brush with egg yolk and bake for 15 minutes, or until brown and puffed. Swap the trays around after 10 minutes. Cover loosely with foil if browning too much. Serve hot.

PREPARATION TIME: 45 MINUTES +   COOKING TIME: 15 MINUTES

THYME TWISTS

2 sheets ready-rolled puff pastry, thawed
1 egg, lightly beaten
thyme leaves, to sprinkle

MAKES 12

Preheat the oven to 210°C (415°F/Gas 6–7). Lightly grease a baking tray with oil or melted butter.

Lay a sheet of pastry on a work surface and brush lightly with beaten egg. Sprinkle the thyme leaves over the pastry. Gently press onto the pastry and top with the second sheet of pastry.

Cut the pastry into twelve 2 cm (¾ inch) strips. Holding both ends, twist the strip in opposite directions twice. Put on the baking tray and bake for 10–15 minutes, or until puffed and golden.

PREPARATION TIME: 10 MINUTES   COOKING TIME: 15 MINUTES

FISH WELLINGTON

40 g (1½ oz) butter
3 onions, thinly sliced
2 x 300 g (10½ oz) skinless firm white fish fillets (each 30 cm/12 inches long)
½ teaspoon sweet paprika
2 red capsicums (peppers), quartered, seeded and membrane removed
1 large eggplant (aubergine) (320 g/11¼ oz), cut into 1 cm (½ inch) thick slices
375 g (13 oz) block puff pastry, thawed
35 g (1¼ oz/⅓ cup) dry breadcrumbs
1 egg, lightly beaten
250 g (9 oz/1 cup) plain yoghurt
1–2 tablespoons chopped dill

SERVES 6

Melt the butter in a saucepan, add the sliced onion and stir to coat. Cover and cook over low heat, stirring occasionally, for 15 minutes. Uncover and cook, stirring, for 15 minutes, or until the onion is very soft and lightly browned. Cool, then season to taste.

Rub one side of each fish fillet with paprika. Place one on top of the other, with the paprika on the outside. If the fillets have a thin and a thick end, sandwich together so the thickness is even along the length (thin ends on top of thick ends).

Cook the capsicum quarters, skin side up, under a hot grill (broiler) until the skin blackens and blisters. Cool in a plastic bag, then peel. Place the eggplant on a greased baking tray and brush with oil. Sprinkle with salt and pepper. Grill until golden, then turn to brown the other side.

Preheat the oven to 220°C (425°F/Gas 7). Roll the pastry out on a lightly floured surface until large enough to enclose the fish, about 25 x 35 cm (10 x 14 inches). The pastry size and shape will be determined by the fish. Sprinkle the breadcrumbs lengthways along the centre of the pastry and place the fish over the breadcrumbs. Top with the onion, then a layer of capsicum, followed by a layer of eggplant.

Brush the pastry edges with beaten egg. Fold the pastry over, pinching firmly together to seal. Use any trimmings to decorate. Brush with egg, then bake for 30 minutes. Cover loosely with foil if the pastry is overbrowning. Slice to serve.

Mix the yoghurt and dill with a little salt and pepper in a bowl. Serve with the Wellington.

PREPARATION TIME: 30 MINUTES COOKING TIME: 1 HOUR 15 MINUTES

CORNISH PASTIES

SHORTCRUST PASTRY

310 g (11 oz/2$\frac{1}{2}$ cups) plain (all-purpose) flour
125 g (4$\frac{1}{2}$ oz) chilled butter, cubed
80–100 ml (2$\frac{1}{2}$–3$\frac{1}{2}$ fl oz) iced water

165 g (5$\frac{3}{4}$ oz) round steak, finely chopped
1 small potato, finely chopped
1 small onion, finely chopped
1 small carrot, finely chopped
1–2 teaspoons worcestershire sauce
2 tablespoons beef stock
1 egg, lightly beaten

MAKES 6

Lightly grease a baking tray. Sift the flour and a pinch of salt into a large bowl. Using your fingertips, rub in the butter until the mixture resembles fine breadcrumbs. Make a well in the centre and add almost all the water. Mix together with a flat-bladed knife, using a cutting action, until the mixture comes together in beads. Add more water if the dough is too dry. Turn out onto a lightly floured work surface and form into a ball. Cover with plastic wrap and refrigerate for 20 minutes.

Preheat the oven to 210°C (415°F/Gas 6–7). Mix together the steak, potato, onion, carrot, worcestershire sauce and stock in a bowl and season well.

Divide the dough into six portions. Roll out each portion to 3 mm ($\frac{1}{8}$ inch) thick. Using a 16 cm (6$\frac{1}{4}$ inch) diameter plate as a guide, cut six circles. Divide the filling among the circles.

Brush the edges with beaten egg and bring the pastry together to form a semi-circle. Pinch the edges into a frill and place on the tray. Brush the pastry with betaen egg and bake for 15 minutes. Reduce the oven to 180°C (350°F/Gas 4) and cook for 25–30 minutes, or until golden.

PREPARATION TIME: 35 MINUTES +   COOKING TIME: 45 MINUTES

TOMATO AND EGGPLANT BOREK

80 g (2³/4 oz) butter, melted
80 ml (2¹/2 fl oz/¹/3 cup) olive oil
185 g (6¹/2 oz/1¹/2 cups) plain (all-purpose) flour

FILLING
250 g (9 oz) tomatoes
2 teaspoons olive oil
1 small onion, chopped
¹/2 teaspoon ground cumin
300 g (10¹/2 oz) eggplant (aubergine), cut into 2 cm (³/4 inch) cubes
2 teaspoons tomato paste (concentrated purée)
1 tablespoon chopped coriander (cilantro)
1 egg, lightly beaten

MAKES 30

Put the butter, oil and 80 ml (2¹/2 fl oz/¹/3 cup) water into a bowl. Season well with salt. Gradually add the flour in batches, mixing with a wooden spoon to form an oily, lumpy dough that comes away from the side of the bowl. Knead gently to bring the dough together, cover with plastic wrap and refrigerate for 1 hour.

Score a cross in the base of each tomato. Put in a heatproof bowl and cover with boiling water. Leave for 30 seconds, then transfer to cold water, drain and peel away the skin from the cross. Cut the tomatoes in half, scoop out the seeds and chop the flesh.

Heat the oil in a frying pan, add the onion and cook, stirring, over low heat for 2–3 minutes, or until soft. Add the cumin, cook for 1 minute, then add the eggplant and cook, stirring, for 8–10 minutes, or until the eggplant begins to soften. Stir in the tomato and tomato paste. Cook over medium heat for 15 minutes, or until the mixture becomes dry. Stir occasionally. Season and stir in the coriander. Cool.

Preheat the oven to 180°C (350°F/Gas 4). Lightly grease two baking trays.

Roll out half the pastry on a lightly floured surface to 2 mm (¹/16 inch) thick. Using an 8 cm (3¹/4 inch) cutter, cut rounds from the pastry. Spoon 2 level teaspoons of the mixture into the centre of each round, lightly brush the edges with water and fold over the filling, expelling any air. Press firmly and crimp the edge with a fork to seal. Place on the trays and brush with the beaten egg. Bake in the top half of the oven for 25 minutes, or until golden brown and crisp.

PREPARATION TIME: 50 MINUTES +   COOKING TIME: 1 HOUR

OLIVE TWISTS

1 tablespoon capers
4 anchovy fillets
2 tablespoons ready-made olive paste
(tapenade)
2 tablespoons finely chopped parsley
oil, to drizzle
2 sheets ready-rolled puff pastry, thawed

MAKES ABOUT 50

Preheat the oven to 200°C (400°F/Gas 6) and line a large baking tray with baking paper.

Finely chop the capers and anchovy fillets and mix with the olive paste, parsley and a drizzle of oil, to form a smooth paste. Spread the pastry with the paste and cut into 1.5 cm (^{5}/8 inch) strips. Twist each strip about four times and bake for about 5–10 minutes, or until golden brown.

PREPARATION TIME: 20 MINUTES   COOKING TIME: 10 MINUTES

SPICY PUMPKIN PUFFS

1 tablespoon vegetable oil
1 onion, finely chopped
3 fresh or dried curry leaves
1 tablespoon brown mustard seeds
2 teaspoons mild Madras curry powder
^{1}/2 teaspoon chilli powder
^{1}/2 teaspoon ground turmeric
350 g (12 oz) pumpkin (winter squash),
diced
80 g (2^3/4 oz/^{1}/2 cup) frozen peas
185 ml (6 fl oz/^{3}/4 cup) chicken stock
5 sheets ready-rolled puff pastry, thawed
1 egg, lightly beaten

MAKES 20

Heat the oil in a frying pan and cook the onion for 2–3 minutes over moderate heat. Add the curry leaves and mustard seeds and fry for 1–2 minutes, or until the mustard seeds pop. Add the curry powder, chilli powder and turmeric to the pan and stir for about 30 seconds, or until combined.

Add the pumpkin to the pan and stir for 1–2 minutes, or until the pumpkin is well coated with spices. Add the peas and stock to the pan and simmer gently for 8–10 minutes, or until the pumpkin is tender and most of the liquid has evaporated. Remove from the heat and allow to cool completely.

Preheat the oven to 220°C (425°F/Gas 7). Lightly brush two baking trays with oil. Cut four 10 cm (4 inch) circles from each of the pastry sheets and spoon 1 tablespoon of the mixture into the centre of each. Brush the edges with the beaten egg and fold over to enclose the filling. Seal the edges by rolling and folding, or pressing with a fork. Place the puffs on the trays and lightly brush with the remaining beaten egg. Bake for 25–30 minutes, or until puffed and golden.

PREPARATION TIME: 20 MINUTES   COOKING TIME: 50 MINUTES

NOTE: The pumpkin puffs can be made 2 days ahead or frozen for up to 2 months.

LAMB FILO FINGERS

1 tablespoon olive oil
350 g (12 oz) lean minced (ground) lamb
1 small onion, finely chopped
2 garlic cloves, crushed
1 tablespoon ground cumin
1 teaspoon ground ginger
1 teaspoon paprika
1 teaspoon ground cinnamon
pinch saffron threads, soaked in a little warm water
1 teaspoon ready-made harissa
2 tablespoons chopped coriander (cilantro)
2 tablespoons chopped flat-leaf (Italian) parsley
40 g (1^1/$_2$ oz /^{1}/$_4$ cup) pine nuts, toasted (see Note)
1 egg
6 sheets filo pastry
60 g (2^1/$_4$ oz) butter, melted
1 tablespoon sesame seeds

YOGHURT SAUCE
250 g (9 oz/1 cup) plain yoghurt
2 tablespoons chopped mint
1 garlic clove, crushed

MAKES 12

Preheat the oven to 180°C (350°F/Gas 4). Lightly grease a large baking tray.

Heat the oil in a large frying pan, add the lamb and cook for 5 minutes, breaking up any lumps with the back of a wooden spoon. Add the onion and garlic and cook for 1 minute. Add the spices, harissa, chopped coriander and parsley and cook for 1 minute, stirring to combine. Transfer to a sieve and drain to remove the fat. Put the mixture in a bowl and allow to cool slightly. Mix in the pine nuts and egg.

Place a sheet of filo on a flat surface with the shortest side facing you. Cover the remaining sheets with a damp tea towel (dish towel) to prevent them from drying out. Cut the sheet of filo into four equal strips lengthways. Brush one of the strips with melted butter and place another on top. Do the same with the other two pieces. Place 1 tablespoon of the lamb mixture on each at the short end of the filo and roll each up, tucking in the ends to hold the mixture in and form each into a cigar shape. Repeat this process until you have used up all the filo and meat mixture.

Place the lamb fingers on the baking tray. Brush with any remaining melted butter and sprinkle with sesame seeds. Bake for 15 minutes, or until lightly golden.

To make the yoghurt sauce, stir all the ingredients together in a small bowl. Serve the filo fingers warm with the sauce on the side.

PREPARATION TIME: 25 MINUTES   COOKING TIME: 25 MINUTES

NOTE: To toast pine nuts, you can dry-fry them in a frying pan, stirring and watching them constantly so they don't burn.

TUNISIAN BRIK

30 g (1 oz) butter
1 small onion, finely chopped
200 g (7 oz) tinned tuna in oil, drained
1 tablespoon tiny capers, rinsed and chopped
2 tablespoons finely chopped flat-leaf (Italian) parsley
2 tablespoons grated parmesan cheese
6 sheets filo pastry
30 g (1 oz) butter, extra, melted
2 small eggs

SERVES 2

Preheat the oven to 200°C (400°F/Gas 6). Melt the butter in a small frying pan and cook the onion over low heat for 5 minutes, or until soft but not brown. Combine the onion, tuna, capers, parsley and parmesan in a bowl and season.

Cut the filo pastry sheets in half widthways. Layer four of the half sheets together, brushing each with melted butter. Keep the remaining pastry covered with a damp tea towel (dish towel). Spoon half the tuna mixture onto one end of the buttered pastry, leaving a border. Make a well in the centre of the mixture and break an egg into the well, being careful to leave it whole.

Layer two more sheets of filo together, brushing with melted butter, and place on top of the tuna and egg. Fold in the pastry sides, then roll into a firm parcel, keeping the egg whole. Place on a lightly greased baking tray and brush with melted butter. Repeat with the remaining pastry, filling and egg. Bake for 15 minutes, or until the pastry is golden brown. Serve warm or at room temperature.

PREPARATION TIME: 30 MINUTES   COOKING TIME: 20 MINUTES

VOL-AU-VENTS

250 g (9 oz) block ready-made puff pastry, thawed
1 egg, lightly beaten

SAUCE AND FILLING
40 g (1½ oz) butter
2 spring onions (scallions), finely chopped
2 tablespoons plain (all-purpose) flour
375 ml (13 fl oz/1½ cups) milk
your choice of filling (see Note)

MAKES 4

Preheat the oven to 220°C (425°F/Gas 7). Line a baking tray with baking paper. Roll out the pastry to a 20 cm (8 inch) square. Cut four circles of pastry with a 10 cm (4 inch) cutter. Place the rounds onto the tray and cut 6 cm (2½ inch) circles into the centre of the rounds with a cutter, taking care not to cut right through the pastry. Place the baking tray in the refrigerator for 15 minutes.

Using a floured knife blade, 'knock up' the sides of each pastry round by making even indentations about 1 cm (½ inch) apart around the circumference. This should allow even rising of the pastry as it cooks. The dough can be made ahead of time up to this stage and frozen until needed. Carefully brush the pastry with the egg, avoiding the 'knocked up' edge as any glaze spilt on the sides will stop the pastry from rising. Bake for 15–20 minutes, or until the pastry has risen and is golden brown and crisp. Cool on a wire rack. Remove the centre from each pastry circle and pull out and discard any partially cooked pastry from the centre. The pastry can be returned to the oven for 2 minutes to dry out if the centre is undercooked. The pastry cases are now ready to be filled with a hot filling before serving.

To make the sauce, melt the butter in a saucepan, add the spring onion and stir over low heat for 2 minutes, or until soft. Add the flour and stir for 2 minutes, or until lightly golden. Gradually add the milk, stirring until smooth. Stir constantly over medium heat for 4 minutes, or until the mixture boils and thickens. Season well. Remove and stir in your choice of filling (see Note).

PREPARATION TIME: 20 MINUTES +   COOKING TIME: 30 MINUTES

NOTE: Add 350 g (12 oz) of any of the following to your white sauce: sliced, cooked mushrooms; peeled, deveined and cooked prawns; chopped, cooked chicken breast; poached, flaked salmon; cooked and dressed crabmeat; oysters; steamed asparagus spears.

CHEESE PASTRIES

165 g (5³/4 oz) feta cheese, grated
60 g (2¹/4 oz/¹/4 cup) ricotta cheese
2 tablespoons chopped mint
1 egg, lightly beaten
2 spring onions (scallions), finely chopped
2 tablespoons dry breadcrumbs
4 sheets ready-rolled puff pastry, thawed
1 egg, extra, lightly beaten
1 tablespoon sesame seeds

MAKES 16

Preheat the oven to 220°C (425°F/Gas 7). Lightly grease two baking trays.

Put the feta, ricotta, mint, egg, spring onion, breadcrumbs and ¹/2 teaspoon cracked black pepper in a bowl and mix with a fork to combine and break up the ricotta.

Using a pastry cutter or saucer, cut 10 cm (4 inch) rounds from the pastry sheets. Spoon level tablespoons of the cheese mixture into the centre of each round and lightly brush the edges with water. Fold over to enclose the filling, expelling any air, and firmly seal with the prongs of a fork to form a crescent shape. Brush with the extra egg and sprinkle with sesame seeds.

Put the crescents on the baking trays and bake for 15–20 minutes, or until well browned and puffed. Serve hot.

PREPARATION TIME: 40 MINUTES   COOKING TIME: 20 MINUTES

ASPARAGUS BOATS

3 sheets ready-rolled shortcrust (pie) pastry, thawed
2 garlic cloves, crushed
1 small onion, finely chopped
30 g (1 oz) butter
2 eggs, lightly beaten
185 g (6¹/2/³/4 cup oz) sour cream
35 g (1¹/4 oz/¹/3 cup) freshly grated parmesan cheese
24 thin asparagus spear tips, blanched (halved if too thick)

MAKES 24

Preheat the oven to 200°C (400°F/Gas 6). Lightly grease twenty-four 8 cm (3¹/4 inch) metal boat-shaped tins. Cut the pastry into 25 cm (10 inch) squares. Cut at 6 cm (2¹/2 inch) intervals to make rectangles, then cut in half. Line the tins with the pastry and chill.

Fry the garlic and onion in the butter until soft. Cool, then stir in the eggs, sour cream and parmesan, then season. Spoon into the boats and place on baking trays. Bake for 15 minutes, or until golden. Top with the blanched asparagus.

PREPARATION TIME: 25 MINUTES +   COOKING TIME: 20 MINUTES

CURRIED PORK AND VEAL SAUSAGE ROLLS

3 sheets ready-rolled puff pastry, thawed
2 eggs, lightly beaten
3 dried Chinese mushrooms
1 tablespoon oil
4 spring onions (scallions), finely chopped
1 garlic clove, crushed
1 small red chilli, finely chopped
2–3 teaspoons curry powder
750 g (1 lb 10 oz) minced (ground) pork and veal
80 g (2³/₄ oz/1 cup) fresh breadcrumbs
1 egg, extra, lightly beaten
3 tablespoons chopped coriander (cilantro)
1 tablespoon soy sauce
1 tablespoon oyster sauce

MAKES 36

Preheat the oven to 200°C (400°F/Gas 6). Lightly grease two baking trays.

Cut the pastry sheets in half and lightly brush the edges with some of the beaten egg. Soak the mushrooms in hot water for 30 minutes, squeeze dry and chop finely.

Heat the oil in a frying pan and cook the spring onions, garlic, chilli and curry powder. Transfer to a bowl and mix with the pork and veal, breadcrumbs, mushrooms, extra egg, coriander, soy sauce and oyster sauce.

Divide into six even portions. Pipe or spoon the filling down the centre of each piece of pastry, then brush the edges with some of the egg. Fold the pastry over the filling, overlapping the edges and placing the join underneath. Brush the rolls with more of the egg, then cut each into six short pieces.

Cut two small slashes on top of each roll. Place the rolls on the trays and bake for 15 minutes, then reduce the oven to 180°C (350°F/Gas 4) and bake for another 15 minutes, or until puffed and golden.

PREPARATION TIME: 30 MINUTES   COOKING TIME: 35 MINUTES

BEEF SAMOSAS WITH MINT CHUTNEY DIP

1 tomato
2 tablespoons oil
1 onion, finely chopped
2 teaspoons finely chopped fresh ginger
400 g (14 oz) minced (ground) beef
1 tablespoon curry powder
1 potato, cubed
1 tablespoon finely chopped mint
6 sheets ready-rolled puff pastry, thawed
1 egg yolk, lightly beaten
1 tablespoon pouring (whipping) cream

MINT CHUTNEY DIP
20 g ($^3/_4$ oz) mint leaves
4 spring onions (scallions)
1 red chilli, seeded
1 tablespoon lemon juice
2 teaspoons caster (superfine) sugar
$^1/_4$ teaspoon garam masala

MAKES ABOUT 20

Score a cross in the base of the tomato. Put in a heatproof bowl and cover with boiling water. Leave for 30 seconds, then transfer to cold water, drain and peel away the skin from the cross. Cut the tomato in half, scoop out the seeds and chop the flesh.

Heat the oil in a pan, add the onion and ginger and cook over medium heat for 3–5 minutes, or until the onion is soft.

Add the beef and curry powder and stir over high heat until the beef has browned. Add 1 teaspoon salt and the tomato and cook, covered, for 5 minutes. Add the potato and 60 ml (2 fl oz/$^1/_4$ cup) water and cook, stirring, for 5 minutes. Remove from the heat, then cool. Stir in the mint.

Preheat the oven to 210°C (415°F/Gas 6–7). Cut the pastry into 13 cm (5 inch) circles using a cutter or small plate as a guide, then cut in half. Form cones by folding each in half and pinching the sides together.

Spoon 2 teaspoons of the beef mixture into each cone. Pinch the top edges together to seal. Place on a lightly greased baking tray. Beat the egg yolk with the cream and brush over the pastry. Bake for 10–15 minutes, or until puffed and golden brown. Serve with mint chutney dip.

To make the dip, roughly chop the mint leaves, spring onion and chilli and place in a food processor or blender with 60 ml (2 fl oz/$^1/_4$ cup) water, $^1/_4$ teaspoon salt and the remaining ingredients. Mix thoroughly and serve with the hot samosas.

PREPARATION TIME: 50 MINUTES COOKING TIME: 30 MINUTES

NOTE: Prepare the samosas up to a day ahead and refrigerate. Cook just before serving. The dip can be made and refrigerated a day ahead.

SWEET POTATO, FETA AND PINE NUT STRUDEL

450 g (1 lb) sweet potato, cut into 2 cm (3/4 inch) cubes
1 tablespoon olive oil
80 g (2 3/4 oz/1/2 cup) pine nuts, toasted (see Notes)
250 g (9 oz) feta cheese, crumbled
2 tablespoons chopped basil
4 spring onions (scallions), chopped
40 g (1 1/2 oz) butter, melted
2 tablespoons olive oil, extra, for brushing
7 sheets filo pastry
2–3 teaspoons sesame seeds

SERVES 6

Preheat the oven to 180°C (350°F/Gas 4). Brush the sweet potato with oil and bake for 20 minutes, or until softened and slightly coloured. Transfer to a bowl and cool slightly.

Add the pine nuts, feta, basil and spring onion to the bowl, mix gently and season to taste.

Mix the butter and extra oil. Remove one sheet of filo and cover the rest with a damp tea towel (dish towel) to prevent them from drying out. Brush each sheet of filo with the butter mixture and layer them into a pile.

Spread the prepared filling in the centre of the filo, covering an area about 10 x 30 cm (4 x 12 inches). Fold the sides of the pastry into the centre, then tuck in the ends. Carefully turn the strudel over and place on a baking tray, seam side down. Lightly brush the top with the butter mixture and sprinkle with sesame seeds. Bake for 35 minutes, or until the pastry is crisp and golden. Serve warm.

PREPARATION TIME: 25 MINUTES   COOKING TIME: 55 MINUTES

NOTES: You can use 450 g (1 lb) of pumpkin (winter squash) instead of the sweet potato.

To toast pine nuts, dry-fry them in a frying pan, stirring and watching them constantly so they don't burn.

CHUTNEY CHICKEN SAUSAGE ROLLS

3 sheets ready-rolled puff pastry, thawed
2 eggs, lightly beaten
750 g (1 lb 10 oz) minced (ground) chicken
4 spring onions (scallions), finely chopped
80 g (2³/₄ oz/1 cup) fresh breadcrumbs
1 carrot, finely grated
2 tablespoons fruit chutney
1 tablespoon sweet chilli sauce
1 tablespoon grated fresh ginger
sesame seeds, to sprinkle

MAKES 36

Preheat the oven to 200°C (400°F/Gas 6). Lightly grease two baking trays. Cut the pastry sheets in half and lightly brush the edges with some of the beaten egg.

Mix half the remaining egg with the remaining ingredients in a large bowl, then divide the mixture into six even portions. Pipe or spoon the filling down the centre of each piece of pastry, then brush the edges with some of the egg. Fold the pastry over the filling, overlapping the edges and placing the join underneath. Brush the rolls with more egg, then cut each into six short pieces. Sprinkle with sesame seeds.

Cut two small slashes on top of each roll and place on the trays. Bake for 15 minutes. Reduce the oven to 180°C (350°F/Gas 4) and bake for another 15 minutes, or until puffed and golden.

PREPARATION TIME: 30 MINUTES   COOKING TIME: 30 MINUTES

TURKEY FILO PARCELS

20 g (³/₄ oz) butter
200 g (7 oz) button mushrooms, sliced
4 bacon slices, diced
350 g (12 oz) cooked turkey, chopped
150 g (5¹/₂ oz) ricotta cheese
2 spring onions (scallions), sliced
3 tablespoons shredded basil
24 sheets filo pastry
butter, extra, melted, for brushing
sesame seeds, to sprinkle

MAKES 24

Melt the butter in a large saucepan and add the mushrooms and bacon. Cook over high heat for 5 minutes, or until the mushrooms are soft and there is no liquid left. Combine the turkey, ricotta, spring onion and basil in a bowl, add the mushroom mixture, then season to taste.

Preheat the oven to 180°C (350°F/Gas 4). Lightly grease a baking tray. Cover the pastry with a damp tea towel (dish towel) to prevent it from drying out. Working with three sheets at a time, brush each layer with melted butter. Cut into three strips. Place 1 tablespoon of filling at the end of each strip and fold the pastry over to form a triangle. Fold until you reach the end of the pastry. Repeat with the remaining pastry and filling. Place on the baking tray, brush with butter and sprinkle with sesame seeds. Bake for 30–35 minutes, or until golden.

PREPARATION TIME: 35 MINUTES   COOKING TIME: 40 MINUTES

TAHINI AND CHILLI PALMIERS

135 g (4³/4 oz/¹/2 cup) tahini
1 red chilli, seeded and finely chopped
¹/2 teaspoon paprika
2 sheets ready-rolled puff pastry, thawed

MAKES 32

Preheat the oven to 200ºC (400ºF/Gas 6). Put the tahini, chilli and paprika in a bowl, season with some salt and stir to combine. Spread half the paste evenly over each pastry sheet, making sure the paste goes all the way to the edges.

Take one pastry sheet and fold from opposite sides until the folds meet in the middle. Then fold one side over the other to resemble a closed book. Repeat with the remaining pastry sheet and tahini mixture. Refrigerate the pastry at this stage for at least 30 minutes, to firm it up and make it easier to work with.

Cut the pastry into 1 cm (¹/2 inch) slices. Cover two baking trays with baking paper and place the palmiers on them, making sure that the palmiers are not too close to one another as they will spread during cooking.

Bake the palmiers for 10–12 minutes on one side, then flip them over and bake for another 5–6 minutes, or until golden and cooked through. They are delicious served at room temperature or cold.

PREPARATION TIME: 25 MINUTES + COOKING TIME: 20 MINUTES

BAKLAVA FINGERS

FILLING
90 g (3¹/4 oz/³/4 cup) walnut pieces, finely
chopped
1 tablespoon soft brown sugar
1 teaspoon ground cinnamon
20 g (³/4 oz) unsalted butter, melted

8 sheets filo pastry
50 g (1³/4 oz) unsalted butter, melted

SYRUP
220 g (7³/4 oz/1 cup) sugar
2 tablespoons honey
2 teaspoons orange flower water
(optional)

MAKES 24

Preheat the oven to 210°C (415°F/Gas 6-7). Brush a baking tray with oil or melted butter.

To make the filling, put the walnuts, sugar, cinnamon and butter in a small bowl and stir until combined.

Remove one sheet of filo and cover the rest with a damp tea towel (dish towel) to prevent them from drying out. Place the sheet of filo pastry on a work bench, brush with melted butter and fold in half. Cut the sheet into three strips and place a heaped teaspoon of filling close to the front edge of the pastry. Roll up, tucking in the edges. Place on the prepared tray and brush with melted butter.

Repeat with the remaining pastry sheets. Bake for 15 minutes, or until golden brown.

To make the syrup, combine the sugar, honey and 125 ml (4 fl oz/¹/2 cup) water in a small saucepan. Stir over low heat, without boiling, until the sugar has completely dissolved. Bring to the boil, reduce the heat and simmer for 5 minutes. Remove from the heat and add the orange flower water.

Transfer to a wire rack over a tray and spoon the syrup over the pastries while both the pastries and syrup are still warm.

PREPARATION TIME: 30 MINUTES   COOKING TIME: 25 MINUTES

NOTE: Store in an airtight container for up to 2 days.

ALMOND FILO SNAKE

70 g (2¹/₂ oz/²/₃ cup) ground almonds
30 g (1 oz/¹/₃ cup) flaked almonds
175 g (6 oz) icing (confectioners') sugar
1 egg, separated
1 teaspoon finely grated lemon zest
¹/₄ teaspoon natural almond extract
1 tablespoon rosewater
2 tablespoons olive oil
2 tablespoons almond oil
9 sheets filo pastry
pinch ground cinnamon
icing (confectioners') sugar, extra, to dust

SERVES 8

Preheat the oven to 180°C (350°F/Gas 4). Lightly grease a 20 cm (8 inch) round spring-form tin.

Put all of the almonds in a bowl with the icing sugar. Put the egg white in a bowl and lightly beat with a fork. Add to the almonds with the lemon zest, almond extract and rosewater. Mix to a paste.

Divide the mixture into three and roll each portion into a sausage 45 cm (17³/₄ inches) long and 1 cm (¹/₂ inch) thick. If the paste is too sticky to roll, dust the bench with icing sugar.

Mix the oils in a bowl. Remove one sheet of filo and cover the rest with a damp tea towel (dish towel) to prevent them from drying out. Brush the filo sheet with the oils, then cover with two more oiled sheets. Place one almond 'sausage' along the length of the oiled pastry and roll up to enclose the filling. Form into a coil and sit the coil in the centre of the tin. Use oil to join the other sausages and continue shaping to make a large coil.

Add the cinnamon to the egg yolk and brush over the snake. Bake for 30 minutes, then remove the side of the tin and turn the snake over. Bake for another 10 minutes to crisp the base. Dust with icing sugar and serve warm.

PREPARATION TIME: 30 MINUTES   COOKING TIME: 40 MINUTES

NOTE: The snake will keep for up to 3 days but should not be refrigerated.

MILLE FEUILLE

600 g (1 lb 5 oz) block ready-made puff pastry or 3 sheets ready-rolled, thawed
625 ml (21/2 fl oz/21/2 cups) thick (double/heavy) cream
500 g (1 lb 2 oz) small strawberries, halved
70 g (21/2 oz) blueberries (optional)

SERVES 6–8

Preheat the oven to 220°C (425°F/Gas 7). Line a baking tray with baking paper. If using a block of puff pastry, cut the pastry into three and roll out to 25 cm (10 inch) squares. Place one sheet of puff pastry on the tray, prick all over and top with another piece of baking paper and another baking tray and bake for 15 minutes. Turn the trays over and bake on the other side for 10-15 minutes, or until golden brown. Allow to cool and repeat with the remaining pastry.

Trim the edges of each pastry sheet and cut each one in half. Pour the cream into a large bowl and whisk to firm peaks. Place two of the pastry pieces on a serving dish and spoon some of the cream on top. Carefully arrange some of the strawberries and blueberries over the cream, pressing them well down. Top each one with another pastry sheet and repeat with the cream, strawberries and blueberries. Top with a final layer of pastry and dust with icing sugar.

PREPARATION TIME: 30 MINUTES   COOKING TIME: 1 HOUR 30 MINUTES

APPLE GALETTES

250 g (9 oz/2 cups) plain (all-purpose) flour
250 g (9 oz) unsalted butter, chopped
125 ml (4 fl oz/1/2 cup) iced water
8 apples, peeled, cored and thinly sliced
175 g (6 oz/3/4 cup) caster (superfine) sugar
125 g (41/2 oz) unsalted butter, chopped

SERVES 8

Put the flour and butter in a bowl and cut the butter into the flour with two knives until it resembles large crumbs. Gradually add the iced water, stirring with a knife and pressing together, until a rough dough forms. Turn onto a lightly floured board and roll into a rectangle. (The dough will be crumbly and hard to manage at this point.) Fold the pastry into thirds — turn it so the hinge is on your left and roll into a large rectangle. Always turn the pastry the same way so the hinge is on the left. Refrigerate in plastic wrap for 30 minutes. Complete two more turns and folds before refrigerating the pastry for another 30 minutes. Repeat the process so that you have completed six folds and turns. Wrap the pastry in plastic wrap and refrigerate before use. The pastry can be stored in the refrigerator for 2 days or in the freezer for up to 3 months.

Preheat the oven to 190°C (375°F/Gas 5). Roll the pastry out on a lightly floured surface until 3 mm (1/8 inch) thick. Cut into eight 10 cm (4 inch) rounds. Arrange the apple in a spiral on the pastry. Sprinkle well with sugar and dot with unsalted butter. Bake on greased baking trays for 20-30 minutes, until the pastry is crisp and golden. Serve warm.

PREPARATION TIME: 45 MINUTES +   COOKING TIME: 30 MINUTES

SHREDDED PASTRIES WITH ALMONDS

500 g (1 lb 2 oz) kataifi pastry (see Note)
250 g (9 oz) unsalted butter, melted
125 g (4^1/$_2$ oz) ground pistachio nuts
200 g (7 oz) ground almonds
575 g (1 lb 4^1/$_2$ oz/2^1/$_2$ cups) caster (superfine) sugar
1 teaspoon ground cinnamon
^{1}/$_4$ teaspoon ground cloves
1 tablespoon brandy
1 egg white
1 teaspoon lemon juice
5 cm (2 inch) strip lemon zest
4 whole cloves
1 cinnamon stick
1 tablespoon honey

MAKES 40 PIECES

Allow the kataifi pastry to come to room temperature, still in its packaging. This will take about 2 hours and makes the pastry easier to work with.

Preheat the oven to 170°C (325°/Gas 3). Brush a 20 x 30 cm (8 x 12 inch) ovenproof dish or tray with some melted butter.

Put the nuts in a bowl with 115 g (4 oz/^{1}/$_2$ cup) of the caster sugar, the ground cinnamon, ground cloves and brandy. Lightly beat the egg white and add to the mixture. Stir to make a paste. Divide the mixture into eight portions and form each into a sausage shape about 18 cm (7 inches) long.

Take a small handful of the pastry strands and spread them out fairly compactly with the strands running lengthways towards you. The pastry should measure 18 x 25 cm (7 x 10 inches). Brush the pastry with melted butter. Place one of the 'nut' sausages along the end of the pastry nearest to you and roll up into a neat sausage shape. Repeat with the other pastry portions.

Place the rolls close together in the dish and brush them again with melted butter. Bake for 50 minutes, or until golden brown.

While the pastries are cooking, put the remaining sugar in a small saucepan with 500 ml (17 fl oz/2 cups) water and stir over low heat until dissolved. Add the lemon juice, lemon zest, whole cloves and cinnamon stick and boil together for 10 minutes. Stir in the honey, then set aside until cold.

When the pastries come out of the oven, pour the syrup over the top. Leave them to cool completely before cutting each roll into five pieces.

PREPARATION TIME: 45 MINUTES +   COOKING TIME: 50 MINUTES

NOTES: Kataifi, a shredded pastry, is available from Greek delicatessens and other speciality food stores.

It is very important that the syrup is cold and the kataifi hot when pouring the syrup over, otherwise the liquid will not be absorbed as well or as evenly.

These pastries keep for up to a week if you cover them. Don't refrigerate them.

DANISH PASTRIES

2 teaspoons dried yeast
125 ml (4 fl oz/$\frac{1}{2}$ cup) warm milk
1 teaspoon caster (superfine) sugar
250 g (9 oz/2 cups) plain
(all-purpose) flour
55 g (2 oz/$\frac{1}{4}$ cup) caster (superfine)
sugar, extra
1 egg, lightly beaten
1 teaspoon natural vanilla extract
250 g (9 oz) unsalted butter, chilled

PASTRY CREAM
2 tablespoons caster (superfine) sugar
2 egg yolks
2 teaspoons plain (all-purpose) flour
2 teaspoons cornflour (cornstarch)
125 ml (4 fl oz/$\frac{1}{2}$ cup) hot milk

425 g (15 oz) tinned apricot halves,
drained
1 egg, lightly beaten
40 g (1$\frac{1}{2}$ oz) flaked almonds
80 g (2$\frac{3}{4}$ oz/$\frac{1}{4}$ cup) apricot jam, to glaze

MAKES 12

Stir the yeast, milk and sugar together in a small bowl until dissolved. Leave in a warm, draught-free place for 10 minutes, or until bubbles appear on the surface. The mixture should be frothy and slightly increased in volume. If your yeast doesn't foam, it is dead, so you will have to discard it and start again. Sift the flour and $\frac{1}{2}$ teaspoon salt into a large bowl and stir in the extra sugar. Make a well in the centre and add the yeast, egg and vanilla. Mix to a firm dough. Turn out onto a lightly floured surface and knead for 10 minutes to form a smooth, elastic dough. Place the dough in a lightly greased bowl, cover and set aside in a warm place for 1 hour, or until doubled in size. Meanwhile, roll the cold butter between two sheets of baking paper to a 15 x 20 cm (6 x 8 inch) rectangle and then refrigerate until required.

Punch down the dough (one punch with your fist) and knead for 1 minute. Roll out to a rectangle measuring 25 x 30 cm (10 x 12 inches). Put the butter in the centre of the dough and fold up the bottom and top of the dough over the butter to join in the centre. Seal the edges with a rolling pin. Give the dough a quarter turn clockwise then roll out to a 20 x 45 cm (8 x 17$\frac{3}{4}$ inch) rectangle. Fold over the top third of the pastry, then the bottom third and then give another quarter turn clockwise. Cover and refrigerate for 30 minutes. Repeat the rolling, folding, turning and chilling four more times. Wrap in plastic wrap and chill for at least another 2 hours.

To make the pastry cream, put the sugar, egg yolks and flours in a saucepan and whisk to combine. Pour the hot milk over the flour and whisk until smooth. Bring to the boil over moderate heat, stirring all the time, until the mixture boils and thickens. Cover and set aside.

Preheat the oven to 200°C (400°F/Gas 6) and line two baking trays with baking paper. On a lightly floured surface, roll the dough into a rectangle or square 3 mm ($\frac{1}{8}$ inch) thick. Cut the dough into 10 cm (4 inch) squares and place on the baking trays. Spoon 1 tablespoon of pastry cream into the centre of each square and top with two apricot halves. Brush one corner with the beaten egg and draw up that corner and the diagonally opposite one to touch in the middle between the apricots. Press firmly in the centre. Leave in a warm place to prove for 30 minutes. Brush each pastry with egg and sprinkle with almonds. Bake for 15–20 minutes, or until golden. Cool on wire racks. Melt the apricot jam with 1 tablespoon water in a saucepan and then strain. Brush the tops of the apricots with the hot glaze and serve.

PREPARATION TIME: 40 MINUTES +   COOKING TIME: 25 MINUTES

PARIS BREST

CHOUX PASTRY
50 g (1³/₄ oz) unsalted butter
90 g (3¹/₄ oz/³/₄ cup) plain (all-purpose) flour, sifted
3 eggs, lightly beaten

FILLING
3 egg yolks
55 g (2 oz/¹/₄ cup) caster (superfine) sugar
2 tablespoons plain (all-purpose) flour
250 ml (9 fl oz/1 cup) milk
1 teaspoon natural vanilla extract
250 ml (9 fl oz/1 cup) pouring (whipping) cream, whipped
200 g (7 oz) raspberries or 250 g (9 oz) strawberries, halved, or a mixture of both

TOPPING
125 g (4¹/₂ oz) dark chocolate, chopped
30 g (1 oz) unsalted butter
1 tablespoon pouring (whipping) cream

SERVES 6–8

Preheat the oven to 210°C (415°F/Gas 6-7). Brush a large tray with melted butter or oil and line the tray with baking paper. Mark a 23 cm (9 inch) circle on the paper.

To make the pastry, stir the butter with 185 ml (6 fl oz/³/₄ cup) water in a saucepan over low heat until the butter has melted and the mixture boils. Remove from the heat, add the flour all at once and, using a wooden spoon, beat until smooth. Return to the heat and beat until the mixture thickens and comes away from the side of the pan. Remove from the heat and cool slightly. Transfer to a large bowl. Using electric beaters, add the eggs gradually, beating until stiff and glossy. Place heaped tablespoons of mixture touching each other, using the marked circle as a guide. Bake for 25–30 minutes, or until browned and hollow sounding when the base is tapped. Turn off the oven and leave the pastry to dry in the oven.

To make the filling, whisk the egg yolks, sugar and flour in a bowl until pale. Heat the milk in a saucepan until almost boiling. Gradually add to the egg mixture, stirring constantly. Return to the pan and stir constantly over medium heat until the mixture boils and thickens. Cook for another 2 minutes, stirring constantly. Remove from the heat and stir in the vanilla extract. Transfer to a bowl, cover the surface with plastic wrap to prevent a skin forming and set aside to cool.

To make the topping, combine all the ingredients in a heatproof bowl. Stand the bowl over a saucepan of simmering water and stir until the chocolate has melted and the mixture is smooth. Cool slightly.

To assemble, cut the pastry ring in half horizontally using a serrated knife. Remove any excess dough that remains in the centre. Fold the whipped cream through the custard and spoon into the base of the pastry. Top with the fruit. Replace the remaining pastry half on top. Using a flat-bladed knife, spread the chocolate mixture over the top of the pastry. Leave to set.

PREPARATION TIME: 50 MINUTES   COOKING TIME: 1 HOUR 15 MINUTES

NOTE: The pastry ring may be made up to 4 hours in advance. Store in an airtight container. The custard may be made up to 4 hours in advance — refrigerate until required. Assemble close to serving time.

APPLE TURNOVERS

500 g (1 lb 2 oz) block ready-made puff
pastry, thawed
1 egg white, lightly beaten
caster (superfine) sugar, to sprinkle

FILLING
200 g (7 oz/1 cup) tinned pie or stewed
apple
1-2 tablespoons caster (superfine) sugar
30 g (1 oz/$^1/_4$ cup) raisins, chopped
30 g (1 oz/$^1/_4$ cup) walnut pieces, chopped

MAKES 12 PIECES

Preheat the oven to 210°C (415°F/Gas 6-7). Lightly grease a baking tray. Roll the pastry on a lightly floured surface to 35 x 45 cm (14 x 17$^3/_4$ inches). Cut out twelve 10 cm (4 inch) rounds.

To make the apple filling, mix together all the ingredients.

Divide the filling among the pastry rounds, then brush the edges with water. Fold in half and pinch firmly together to seal. Use the back of a knife to push up the pastry edge at intervals. Brush the tops with egg white and sprinkle with caster sugar. Make two small slits in the top of each turnover. Bake for 15 minutes, then lower the oven to 190°C (375°F/Gas 5) and bake for 10 minutes, or until golden.

PREPARATION TIME: 40 MINUTES   COOKING TIME: 25 MINUTES

PEACH BAKLAVA

6 sheets filo pastry
60 g (2$^1/_4$ oz) unsalted butter, melted
85 g (3 oz/$^2/_3$ cup) slivered almonds
1$^1/_2$ teaspoons ground cinnamon
100 g (3$^1/_2$ oz/$^1/_2$ cup) soft brown sugar
185 ml (6 fl oz/$^3/_4$ cup) orange juice,
strained
4 peaches, halved and thinly sliced
icing (confectioners') sugar, to dust

SERVES 8

Preheat the oven to 180°C (350°F/Gas 4). Cut each sheet of pastry into eight squares. Line eight 250 ml (9 fl oz/1 cup) muffin holes with three layers of filo pastry, brush the pieces with melted butter to stick them together and overlap the sheets at angles.

Combine the almonds, cinnamon and half the sugar in a small bowl. Sprinkle over the bases then cover with the three final squares of filo pastry brushed with butter. Bake for 10-15 minutes.

Meanwhile, dissolve the remaining sugar in the orange juice, bring to the boil, reduce the heat and simmer. Add the peaches to the syrup and stir gently to coat the fruit. Simmer for 2-3 minutes, then lift from the pan with a slotted spoon. Arrange the peaches on the pastries, dust with icing sugar and serve with clotted cream or ice cream.

PREPARATION TIME: 40 MINUTES   COOKING TIME: 20-25 MINUTES

NOTE: Peaches can be peeled if you like. Tinned peaches can be used instead of fresh.

CROISSANTS

330 ml (11^1/$_4$ fl oz/1^1/$_3$ cups) warm milk
2 teaspoons dried yeast
55 g (2 oz/^{1}/$_4$ cup) caster (superfine) sugar
405 g (14^1/$_4$ oz/3^1/$_4$ cups) plain
(all-purpose) flour
250 g (9 oz) unsalted butter, at room
temperature
1 egg

MAKES 12

Combine the milk, yeast and 1 tablespoon of the sugar in a small bowl and stir until dissolved. Leave in a warm, draught-free place for 10 minutes, or until bubbles appear on the surface. The mixture should be frothy and slightly increased in volume. If your yeast doesn't foam, it is dead, so you will have to discard it and start again.

Put the flour, remaining sugar and 1 teaspoon salt in a large bowl and make a well in the centre. Pour the yeast mixture into the well and mix to a rough dough with a wooden spoon. Turn out onto a floured surface and knead for 10 minutes, or until smooth and elastic. Add only a small amount of flour — just enough to stop the dough sticking. Place in a large greased bowl, cover and set aside in a warm place for 1 hour, or until doubled in bulk.

Meanwhile, place the butter between two sheets of baking paper, cut in half lengthways and use a rolling pin to pat out to a 10 x 20 cm (4 x 8 inch) rectangle. Cover and refrigerate the butter.

Punch down the dough (one punch with your fist). Knead briefly on a lightly floured surface then roll to a rectangle 12 x 45 cm (4^1/$_2$ x 17^3/$_4$ inches). Place the butter on the lower half of the dough and fold down the top half. Seal all around the edges using your fingertips to completely seal in the butter. Turn the folded side of the dough to the right. Roll out the dough to a rectangle about 22 x 45 cm (8^1/$_2$ x 17^3/$_4$ inches), then fold up the bottom third and fold down the top third. Wrap in plastic wrap for 20 minutes. Roll again with the fold to the right. Chill for 20 minutes then repeat the process two more times. The butter should be completely incorporated — roll again if not incorporated.

Lightly brush two baking trays with melted butter. Cut the dough in half. Roll each half into a large rectangle and trim each to about 22 x 36 cm (8^1/$_2$ x 14^1/$_4$ inches). Cut a cardboard triangular template 18 cm (7 inches) across the base and 14 cm (5^1/$_2$ inches) along each side. Cut each rectangle into six triangles. Stretch each triangle a little to extend its length. Roll each triangle into a crescent, starting from the base. Place well apart on the prepared tray, cover and refrigerate for a minimum of 4 hours, or overnight.

Preheat the oven to 200°C (400°F/Gas 6). Lightly beat the egg with 2 teaspoons water in a small bowl. Brush the pastries with the egg glaze and set aside for 40 minutes, or until doubled in bulk. Brush again with egg glaze. Bake for 15–20 minutes, or until crisp and golden.

PREPARATION TIME: 40 MINUTES + COOKING TIME: 20 MINUTES

APPLE STRUDEL

30 g (1 oz) unsalted butter
4 green cooking apples, peeled, cored and thinly sliced
2 tablespoons orange juice
1 tablespoon honey
55 g (2 oz/¼ cup) sugar
60 g (2¼ oz/½ cup) sultanas (golden raisins)
2 sheets ready-rolled puff pastry, thawed
25 g (1 oz/¼ cup) ground almonds
1 egg, lightly beaten
2 tablespoons soft brown sugar
1 teaspoon ground cinnamon

MAKES 2 STRUDELS

Preheat the oven to 220°C (425°F/Gas 7). Brush two oven trays lightly with melted butter or oil. Heat the butter in a saucepan. Add the apple slices and cook for 2 minutes until lightly golden. Add the orange juice, honey, sugar and sultanas. Stir over medium heat until the sugar dissolves and the apple is just tender. Transfer the mixture to a bowl and leave until completely cooled.

Place one sheet of pastry on a flat work surface. Fold it in half and make small cuts in the folded edge of the pastry at 2 cm (¾ inch) intervals. Open out the pastry and sprinkle with half of the ground almonds. Drain away the liquid from the apple and place half of the mixture in the centre of the pastry. Brush the edges with some of the lightly beaten egg, and fold together, pressing firmly to seal.

Place the strudel on a prepared tray, seam side down. Brush the top with egg and sprinkle with half of the combined brown sugar and cinnamon. Repeat the process with the other sheet of pastry, remaining filling and the rest of the brown sugar and cinnamon. Bake for 20-25 minutes, or until the pastry is golden and crisp. Serve hot with cream or ice cream, or at room temperature as a teatime treat.

PREPARATION TIME: 20 MINUTES   COOKING TIME: 30 MINUTES

NOTE: Many types of fresh or tinned fruit, such as pears, cherries or apricots, can be used to make strudel. Just make sure that the fruit is well drained before using, or the pastry base will become soggy.

PROFITEROLES

CHOUX PASTRY

50 g (1^3/$_4$ oz) unsalted butter

90 g (3^1/$_4$ oz/^{3}/$_4$ cup) plain (all-purpose)
flour, sifted twice

3 eggs, lightly beaten

FILLING

375 ml (13 fl oz/1^1/$_2$ cups) milk

4 egg yolks

80 g (2^3/$_4$ oz/^{1}/$_3$ cup) caster
(superfine) sugar

30 g (1 oz/^{1}/$_4$ cup) plain (all-purpose) flour

1 teaspoon natural vanilla extract

110 g (3^3/$_4$ oz) good-quality dark chocolate

2 teaspoons oil

SERVES 10

Preheat the oven to 210°C (415°F/Gas 6-7). Lightly grease two baking trays. To make the pastry, put the butter in a large heavy-based saucepan with 185 ml (6 fl oz/^{3}/$_4$ cup) water and stir over medium heat until the mixture comes to the boil. Remove from the heat and quickly beat in the flour with a wooden spoon. Return to the heat and continue beating until the mixture comes together, forms a ball and leaves the side of the pan. Allow to cool slightly.

Transfer to a bowl and beat to release any remaining heat. Gradually add the beaten egg, about 3 teaspoons at a time, beating well after each addition, until all the egg has been added and the mixture is thick and glossy — a wooden spoon should stand upright in it. If it is too runny, the egg has been added too quickly. If this happens, beat for several more minutes, or until thickened.

Sprinkle the baking trays with water — this creates steam in the oven, helping the puffs to rise. Spoon heaped teaspoons of the mixture onto the baking trays, leaving room for spreading. Bake for 20–30 minutes, or until browned and hollow sounding, then remove and make a small hole in the base of each puff with a skewer. Return to the oven for 5 minutes to dry out. Cool on a wire rack.

To make the filling, put the milk in a small saucepan and bring to the boil. Set aside while quickly whisking the yolks and sugar in a bowl until combined. Whisk the flour into the egg mixture. Pour the hot milk slowly onto the egg and flour mixture, whisking constantly. Wash out the pan, return the milk mixture to the pan and bring to the boil, stirring with a wooden spoon until the mixture comes to the boil and thickens. Transfer to a heatproof bowl and stir in the vanilla extract. Lay plastic wrap directly over the surface to prevent a skin forming, then refrigerate until cold.

Pipe the filling into the profiteroles through the hole in the base, using a piping (icing) bag fitted with a small nozzle.

Chop the chocolate and put it in a heatproof bowl with the oil. Bring a saucepan of water to the boil and remove the saucepan from the heat. Sit the bowl over the saucepan, making sure the base of the bowl does not touch the water. Allow to stand, stirring occasionally, until the chocolate has melted. Stir until smooth and dip the profiterole tops in the chocolate. Allow to set completely before serving.

PREPARATION: 30 MINUTES   COOKING TIME: 1 HOUR

SUGAR AND SPICE PALMIERS

500 g (1 lb 2 oz) ready-made puff pastry, thawed
2 tablespoons sugar
1 teaspoon mixed (pumpkin pie) spice
1 teaspoon ground cinnamon
40 g (1½ oz) unsalted butter, melted
icing (confectioners') sugar, to dust

MAKES 32

Preheat the oven to 210°C (415°F/Gas 6–7). Lightly grease two baking trays, then line with baking paper. Roll out the pastry between two sheets of baking paper to make a 30 cm (12 inch) square 3 mm (⅛ inch) thick. Combine the sugar and spices in a small bowl. Cut the sheet of pastry in half, then brush each pastry sheet with melted butter. Sprinkle with the sugar mixture, reserving 2 teaspoons.

Take one half of pastry, fold the short edges of pastry inwards, so that the edges almost meet in the centre. Fold the same way once more, then fold over and place on baking paper. Repeat with the other half. Refrigerate both portions for 15 minutes. Using a small, sharp knife, cut each half into 16 slices.

Arrange the palmiers, cut side up, on the prepared trays, brush with butter and sprinkle lightly with the reserved sugar mixture. Bake for 20 minutes until golden. Leave to cool on a wire rack. Lightly dust with sifted icing sugar.

PREPARATION TIME: 20 MINUTES +   COOKING TIME: 20 MINUTES

INDIVIDUAL PITHIVIERS

60 g (2¼ oz) unsalted butter
55 g (2 oz/¼ cup) sugar
1 egg
70 g (2½ oz/⅔ cup) ground almonds
1 tablespoon plain (all-purpose) flour
2 teaspoons grated orange zest
1 tablespoon Cointreau
375 g (13 oz) block puff pastry or 4 sheets ready-rolled, thawed
1 egg, lightly beaten

SERVES 8

Preheat the oven to 210°C (415°F/ Gas 6–7). Grease two baking trays and line with baking paper. Using electric beaters, beat the butter and sugar until light and creamy. Add the egg and beat until well combined. Stir in the ground almonds, flour, orange zest and Cointreau. Cover and refrigerate.

Cut the block of puff pastry in half. On a lightly floured surface, roll one half out to a large enough rectangle to cut out eight 10 cm (4 inch) rounds. Carefully transfer to baking trays. Using a smaller round cutter, mark a 7 cm (2¾ inch) impression in the middle of each circle. Divide the nut cream among the pastry circles, spreading evenly inside the marked impression. Brush the edges with beaten egg. Roll out the remaining puff pastry. Using a larger cutter, cut out eight 10 cm (4 inch) circles and place over the top of the filling, pressing the edges to seal. Brush the tops with beaten egg, being careful not to let any drip down the side, as this will prevent the pastry rising. Using the tip of a small knife, score a spiral pattern on the top of each pithivier. Bake for 20–25 minutes, or until puffed and golden.

PREPARATION TIME: 40 MINUTES   COOKING TIME: 25 MINUTES

FEUILLETÉ WITH CHERRIES JUBILEE

375 g (13 oz) block puff pastry, thawed
1 egg, lightly beaten
20 g (³/4 oz) unsalted butter
20 g (³/4 oz) sugar
500 g (1 lb 2 oz) cherries, pitted
300 ml (10¹/2 fl oz) thick (double/heavy) cream
125 ml (4 fl oz/¹/2 cup) brandy or Kirsch
icing (confectioners') sugar, to dust

SERVES 4

To make the feuilletés, roll the pastry out on a floured work surface and cut out four rectangles of 10 x 12 cm (4 x 4¹/2 inches) each. Put them on a baking tray and brush with the beaten egg, being careful not to let any drip down the sides of the pastry. Refrigerate for 30 minutes. Preheat the oven to 220°C (425°F/Gas 7).

Melt the butter and sugar together in a saucepan and add the cherries. Cook over high heat for about 1 minute, then reduce the heat and simmer for about 3 minutes, or until the cherries are tender. Reduce the heat to low and keep the cherries warm.

Bake the feuilletés on the top shelf of the oven for 15 minutes until golden and puffed, then cut them in half horizontally and gently pull any doughy bits out of the centre. Turn the oven off and put the feuilletés back in the oven and allow to dry out for a couple of minutes.

When you are ready to serve, whisk the cream until it reaches stiff peaks. Place a warm feuilleté base on each serving plate. Heat the brandy or Kirsch in a small saucepan and set it alight, then pour it over the cherries (keep a saucepan lid nearby in case the flames get too high). Spoon some cherries into each feuilleté and top with a little cream. Put the lids on and dust with icing sugar before serving.

PREPARATION TIME: 15 MINUTES +   COOKING TIME: 25 MINUTES

JALOUSIE

30 g (1 oz) unsalted butter
50 g (1³/₄ oz/¹/₄ cup) soft brown sugar
500 g (1 lb 2 oz) apples, peeled, cored and cubed
1 teaspoon grated lemon zest
1 tablespoon lemon juice
¹/₄ teaspoon freshly grated nutmeg
¹/₄ teaspoon cinnamon
30 g (1 oz/¹/₄ cup) sultanas (golden raisins)
375 g (13 oz) block puff pastry, thawed
1 egg, lightly beaten, to glaze

SERVES 4–6

Preheat the oven to 220°C (425°F/Gas 7). Lightly grease a baking tray and line with baking paper.

Melt the butter and sugar in a frying pan. Add the apple, lemon zest and lemon juice. Cook over medium heat for 10 minutes, stirring occasionally, until the apples are cooked and the mixture is thick and syrupy. Stir in the nutmeg, cinnamon and sultanas. Cool completely.

Cut the block of puff pastry in half. On a lightly floured surface roll out one half of the pastry to an 18 x 24 cm (7 x 9¹/₂ inch) rectangle. Spread the fruit mixture onto the pastry, leaving a 2.5 cm (1 inch) border. Brush the edges lightly with the beaten egg.

Roll the second half of the pastry on a lightly floured surface to a 18 x 25 cm (7 x 10 inch) rectangle. Using a sharp knife, cut slashes in the pastry across its width, leaving a 2 cm (³/₄ inch) border around the edge. The slashes should open slightly and look like a venetian blind (jalousie in French). Place over the fruit and press the edges together. Trim away any extra pastry. Knock up the puff pastry (brush the sides upwards) with a knife to ensure rising during cooking. Glaze the top with egg. Bake for 25–30 minutes, or until puffed and golden.

PREPARATION TIME: 40 MINUTES   COOKING TIME: 45 MINUTES

BREADS AND PIZZAS

CHALLAH

275 g (9³/₄ oz) boiling potatoes, cubed
2 teaspoons dried yeast
80 ml (2¹/₂ fl oz/¹/₃ cup) oil
2 large eggs
2 large egg yolks
2 tablespoons honey
550 g (1 lb 4 oz/4¹/₂ cups) white strong flour
1 egg yolk, extra
sesame seeds or poppy seeds

MAKES 1 LOAF

Boil the potato in 625 ml (21¹/₂ fl oz/2¹/₂ cups) water for 10 minutes, or until very soft. Drain well, reserving the potato water. Leave to cool for 5 minutes, then mash the potato until very smooth. Grease and lightly flour a baking tray. Put the yeast and 125 ml (4 fl oz/¹/₂ cup) warm water in a small bowl and stir well. Leave in a warm, draught-free place for 10 minutes, or until bubbles appear on the surface. The mixture should be frothy and slightly increased in volume. If your yeast doesn't foam, it is dead, so you will have to discard it and start again.

Put the oil, eggs, egg yolks, honey, 1¹/₂ teaspoons salt, 125 ml (4 fl oz/¹/₂ cup) reserved potato water and the mashed potato in a large bowl and beat with a wooden spoon until smooth. Leave to cool. Add the yeast mixture and gradually mix in 250 g (9 oz/2 cups) of the flour, beating until smooth. Add another 185 g (6¹/₂ oz/1¹/₂ cups) flour and mix until a rough soft dough is formed. Place the dough on a lightly floured work surface. Knead for 10 minutes, or until the dough is smooth. Incorporate the remaining flour, as required, to keep the dough from sticking. Place in an oiled bowl and brush the surface with oil. Cover with plastic wrap or a damp tea towel (dish towel) and leave in a warm place for 1¹/₂ hours, or until doubled in size.

Turn the dough out onto a floured work surface and knead for 4 minutes. Divide the dough into two, a one-third portion and a two-thirds portion, then divide each portion into three equal parts. Leave to rest for 10 minutes. Roll each part into ropes about 35 cm (14 inches) long, with the centre slightly thicker than the ends. Braid the three thicker ropes, pinching the ends together firmly. Place the larger braid on the prepared tray. Whisk the extra egg yolk and 1 tablespoon water and brush some over the surface of the challah. Repeat the process with the remaining three ropes and place on top of the first braid, making sure the ends of the braids overlap. Secure tightly and brush the surface with some of the egg glaze. Cover with plastic wrap and leave in a warm, draught-free place for 30 minutes, or until doubled in size. Preheat the oven to 180°C (350°F/Gas 4).

Brush the dough with the remaining egg glaze and sprinkle with the sesame seeds. Bake for 50–55 minutes, or until golden brown. Cool on a wire rack.

PREPARATION TIME: 1 HOUR +   COOKING TIME: 1 HOUR 5 MINUTES

NOTE: No Shabbat (Jewish Sabbath) dinner would be complete without a loaf of this rich, braided bread.

SOY AND LINSEED LOAF

110 g (3¾ oz/½ cup) pearl barley
2 teaspoons dried yeast
1 teaspoon caster (superfine) sugar
1 tablespoon linseeds (flax seeds)
2 tablespoons soy flour
2 tablespoons gluten flour
150 g (5½ oz/1 cup) wholemeal
(whole-wheat) strong flour
310 g (11 oz/2½ cups) white strong flour
2 tablespoons olive oil

MAKES 1 LOAF

Brush a 10 x 26 cm (4 x 10½ inch) bread tin with oil. Put the barley in a saucepan with 500 ml (17 fl oz/2 cups) water, bring to the boil and boil for 20 minutes, or until softened. Drain.

Put the yeast, sugar and 150 ml (5 fl oz) warm water in a small bowl and mix well. Leave in a warm, draught-free place for 10 minutes, or until bubbles appear on the surface. The mixture should be frothy and slightly increased in volume. If your yeast doesn't foam, it is dead, so you will have to discard it and start again.

Put the barley, linseeds, soy and gluten flours, wholemeal flour, 250 g (9 oz/2 cups) of the white flour and 1 teaspoon salt in a large bowl. Make a well in the centre and add the yeast mixture, oil and 150 ml (5 fl oz) warm water. Mix with a wooden spoon to a soft dough. Turn out onto a floured surface and knead for 10 minutes, or until smooth and elastic. Incorporate enough of the remaining flour until the dough is no longer sticky.

Place in an oiled bowl and brush the dough with oil. Cover with plastic wrap or a damp tea towel (dish towel) and leave in a warm, draught-free place for 45 minutes, or until doubled in size. Punch down and knead for 2–3 minutes.

Pat the dough into a 20 x 24 cm (8 x 9½ inch) rectangle. Roll up firmly from the long side and place, seam side down, in the bread tin. Cover with plastic wrap or a damp tea towel and set aside in a warm, draught-free place for 1 hour, or until risen to the top of the tin. Preheat the oven to 200°C (400°F/Gas 6).

Brush the dough with water and make two slits on top. Bake for 30 minutes, or until golden. Remove from the tin and cool on a wire rack.

PREPARATION TIME: 30 MINUTES +   COOKING TIME: 50 MINUTES

TURKISH BREAD

1 tablespoon dried yeast
$^1/_2$ teaspoon sugar
60 g (2$^1/_4$ oz/$^1/_2$ cup) plain
(all-purpose) flour
440 g (15$^1/_2$ oz/3$^1/_2$ cups) white
strong flour
80 ml (2$^1/_2$ fl oz/$^1/_3$ cup) olive oil
1 egg, lightly beaten with 2 teaspoons
water
nigella or sesame seeds, to sprinkle

MAKES 3 LOAVES

Put the yeast, sugar and 125 ml (4 fl oz/$^1/_2$ cup) warm water in a small bowl and stir well. Add a little of the flour and mix to a paste. Leave in a warm, draught-free place for 10 minutes, or until bubbles appear on the surface. The mixture should be frothy and slightly increased in volume. If your yeast doesn't foam, it is dead, so you will have to discard it and start again.

Put the remaining flours and 1$^1/_2$ teaspoons salt in a large bowl and make a well in the centre. Add the yeast mixture, olive oil and 250 ml (9 fl oz/1 cup) warm water. Mix to a rough dough, then turn out onto a floured surface and knead for 5 minutes. Add minimal flour as the dough should remain damp and springy.

Shape the dough into a ball and place in a large oiled bowl. Cover with plastic wrap or a damp tea towel (dish towel) and leave in a warm place for 1 hour to triple in size. Punch down and divide into three. Knead each portion for 2 minutes and shape each into a ball. Cover with plastic wrap or a damp tea towel and leave for 10 minutes.

Roll each portion of dough into a rectangle 15 x 35 cm (6 x 14 inches). Cover with damp tea towels and leave in a warm place for 20 minutes. Indent all over the surface with your fingers, brush with the egg glaze and sprinkle with the seeds. Preheat the oven to 220°C (425°F/Gas 7).

For the best results, bake each loaf separately. Place a baking tray in the oven for a couple of minutes until hot, remove and sprinkle lightly with flour. Place one portion of dough on the hot tray and bake for 10–12 minutes, or until puffed and golden brown. Wrap in a clean tea towel to soften the crust and set aside to cool. Meanwhile, repeat baking the remaining portions of dough.

PREPARATION TIME: 30 MINUTES +   COOKING TIME: 30 MINUTES

DAMPER

375 g (13 oz/3 cups) self-raising flour
90 g (3^1/4 oz) butter, melted
125 ml (4 fl oz/^{1}/2 cup) milk
milk, extra, to glaze
flour, extra, to dust

MAKES 1 DAMPER

Preheat the oven to 210°C (415°F/Gas 6-7). Grease a baking tray. Sift the flour and 1-2 teaspoons salt into a bowl and make a well in the centre. Combine the butter, milk and 125 ml (4 fl oz/^{1}/2 cup) water and pour into the well. Stir with a knife until just combined. Turn the dough onto a lightly floured surface and knead for 20 seconds, or until smooth. Place the dough on the baking tray and press out to a 20 cm (8 inch) circle.

Using a sharp pointed knife, score the dough into eight sections about 1 cm (^{1}/2 inch) deep. Brush with milk, then dust with flour. Bake for 10 minutes. Reduce the oven to 180°C (350°F/Gas 4) and bake the damper for another 15 minutes, or until the damper is golden and sounds hollow when the surface is tapped. Serve with butter.

PREPARATION TIME: 20 MINUTES   COOKING TIME: 25 MINUTES

NOTE: Damper is the Australian version of soda bread. It is traditionally served warm with slatherings of golden syrup. If you prefer, you can make four rounds instead of one large damper and slightly reduce the cooking time. Cut two slashes in the form of a cross on the top.

BROWN SODA BREAD

250 g (9 oz/2 cups) self-raising flour
250 g (9 oz/2 cups) unbleached self-raising flour
1 teaspoon bicarbonate of soda (baking soda)
750 ml (26 fl oz/3 cups) buttermilk

MAKES 1 LOAF

Preheat the oven to 190°C (375°F/Gas 5). Lightly grease a baking tray. Sift the flours and bicarbonate of soda into a large bowl, add the husks to the bowl and make a well in the centre. Add 625 ml (21^1/2 fl oz/2^1/2 cups) of the buttermilk and mix with a knife to form a soft dough, adding some of the remaining buttermilk if required.

Turn the dough onto a floured surface and knead gently and briefly — don't knead too much as this will make it tough. Press the dough out to a 20 cm (8 inch) round and place on the baking tray. Score a deep cross with a floured knife one-third the depth of the dough. Lightly brush with water and sprinkle with a little flour. Bake for 20–30 minutes, or until the bread sounds hollow when tapped.

PREPARATION TIME: 20 MINUTES   COOKING TIME: 30 MINUTES

SOURDOUGH BREAD

STARTER
125 g (4½ oz/1 cup) white strong flour
2 teaspoons fresh yeast

SPONGE
125 g (4½ oz/1 cup) white strong flour

DOUGH
375 g (13 oz/3 cups) white strong flour
2 teaspoons fresh yeast

MAKES 2 LOAVES

To make the starter, sift the flour into a bowl and make a well in the centre. Cream the yeast and 250 ml (9 fl oz/1 cup) warm water together, pour into the flour and gradually draw the flour into the centre to form a thick smooth paste. Cover with plastic wrap or a damp tea towel (dish towel) and leave at room temperature for 24 hours. The starter will begin to ferment and bubble.

To make the sponge, stir the flour into the starter mixture and gradually whisk in 125 ml (4 fl oz/½ cup) warm water to form a smooth mixture. Cover with plastic wrap and leave for 24 hours.

To make the dough, sift the flour and 1 teaspoon salt into a large bowl and make a well in the centre. Cream the yeast and 80 ml (2½ fl oz/⅓ cup) warm water together and add to the dry ingredients with the starter and sponge mixture. Gradually incorporate the flour into the well. Turn the dough onto a lightly floured surface and knead for 10 minutes, or until smooth and elastic, incorporating extra flour if needed.

Place the dough in a lightly oiled bowl, cover with plastic wrap or a damp tea towel and place in a warm place for 1 hour, or until doubled in size. Lightly grease two baking trays and dust lightly with flour. Punch the dough down and turn onto the work surface. Knead for 1 minute, or until smooth. Divide into two equal portions and shape each into a 20 cm (8 inch) round. Using a sharp knife, score diagonal cuts 1 cm (½ inch) deep along the loaves.

Place the loaves on the trays and cover with plastic wrap or a damp tea towel. Leave in a warm place for 45 minutes, or until doubled in size. Preheat the oven to 190°C (375°F/Gas 5). Bake for 35–40 minutes, changing the breads around halfway through. Bake until the bread is golden and crusty and sounds hollow when tapped. Cool on a wire rack before cutting.

PREPARATION TIME: 30 MINUTES +   COOKING TIME: 40 MINUTES

FLATBREAD WITH ZA'ATAR

1 tablespoon dried yeast
1 teaspoon sugar
405 g (14^1/$_4$ oz/3^1/$_4$ cups) plain
(all-purpose) flour
125 ml (4 fl oz/^{1}/$_2$ cup) olive oil
20 g (^{3}/$_4$ oz/^{1}/$_3$ cup) za'atar (see Note)
1 tablespoon sea salt flakes

MAKES 10

Put the yeast and sugar in a small bowl with 60 ml (2 fl oz/^{1}/$_4$ cup) warm water and stir until dissolved. Leave in a warm, draught-free place for 10 minutes, or until bubbles appear on the surface. The mixture should be frothy and slightly increased in volume. If your yeast doesn't foam, it is dead, so you will have to discard it and start again.

Sift the flour and ^{1}/$_2$ teaspoon salt into a large bowl. Make a well in the centre and pour in the yeast mixture and 310 ml (10^3/$_4$ fl oz/1^1/$_4$ cups) warm water. Gradually combine to form a dough, then knead on a floured surface for 10–15 minutes until smooth and elastic, gradually adding 1 tablespoon olive oil as you knead, until all the oil has been used. Cover and set aside in a warm place for 1 hour, or until risen.

Punch down the dough with your fist and then knead again. Set aside and leave to rise for 30 minutes. Knead briefly and divide into 10 portions. Roll each portion to a smooth circle about 5 mm (^{1}/$_4$ inch) thick. Set aside covered with a tea towel (dish towel) for another 20 minutes.

Preheat the oven to 220°C (425°F/Gas 7). Grease two baking trays. Place the rolls on the trays and gently press the surface with your fingers to create a dimpled effect. Brush with the remaining oil and sprinkle with za'atar and sea salt flakes. Bake for 12–15 minutes. Serve warm.

PREPARATION TIME: 35 MINUTES +   COOKING TIME: 15 MINUTES

NOTE: Za'atar mix is a Middle Eastern spice blend of toasted sesame seeds, dried thyme, dried majoram and sumac. It is available from speciality food stores.

FOCACCIA

2 teaspoons dried yeast
1 teaspoon caster (superfine) sugar
2 tablespoons olive oil
405 g (14^1/$_4$ oz/3^1/$_4$ cups) white strong flour
1 tablespoon full-cream milk powder

TOPPING
1 tablespoon olive oil
1-2 garlic cloves, crushed
black olives
rosemary sprigs or leaves
1 teaspoon dried oregano
1-2 teaspoons coarse sea salt

MAKES 1 FLAT LOAF

Lightly grease a 18 x 28 cm (7 x 11^1/$_4$ inch) baking tin. Put the yeast, sugar and 250 ml (9 fl oz/1 cup) warm water in a small bowl and stir well. Leave in a warm, draught-free place for 10 minutes, or until bubbles appear on the surface. The mixture should be frothy and slightly increased in volume. If your yeast doesn't foam, it is dead, so you will have to discard it and start again. Add the oil.

Sift 375 g (13 oz/3 cups) of the flour, the milk powder and ^{1}/$_2$ teaspoon salt into a large bowl. Make a well in the centre and add the yeast mixture. Beat with a wooden spoon until the mixture is well combined. Add enough of the remaining flour to form a soft dough, and then turn onto a lightly floured surface.

Knead for 10 minutes, or until the dough is smooth and elastic. Place the dough in a large, lightly oiled bowl. Brush the surface of the dough with oil. Cover with plastic wrap or a damp tea towel (dish towel) and leave in a warm place for 1 hour, or until well risen. Punch down the dough and knead for 1 minute. Roll into a rectangle, 18 x 28 cm (7 x 11^1/$_4$ inches) and place in the prepared tin. Cover with plastic wrap and leave to rise in a warm place for 20 minutes. Using the handle of a wooden spoon, form indents 1 cm (^{1}/$_2$ inch) deep all over the dough at regular intervals. Cover with plastic wrap and set aside for 30 minutes, or until the dough is well risen. Preheat the oven to 180°C (350°F/Gas 4).

To make the topping, brush the combined olive oil and garlic over the surface of the dough. Top with the olives and rosemary sprigs, then sprinkle with the oregano and salt.

Bake for 20-25 minutes, or until golden and crisp. Cut into large squares and serve warm.

PREPARATION TIME: 50 MINUTES +   COOKING TIME: 25 MINUTES

NOTES: Focaccia is best eaten on the day of baking. It can be reheated if necessary.

UNLEAVENED LAVASH

125 g (4$\frac{1}{2}$ oz/1 cup) plain (all-purpose) flour
$\frac{1}{2}$ teaspoon sugar
20 g ($\frac{3}{4}$ oz) chilled butter, chopped
80 ml (2$\frac{1}{2}$ fl oz/$\frac{1}{3}$ cup) milk
sesame and poppy seeds, to sprinkle

MAKES 4

Put the flour, sugar, butter and $\frac{1}{2}$ teaspoon salt in a food processor. Process in short bursts until the butter is incorporated. With the machine running, gradually pour in the milk and process until the dough comes together — you may need to add an extra 1 tablespoon milk. Turn out onto a lightly floured surface and knead briefly until smooth. Wrap in plastic wrap and refrigerate for 1 hour.

Preheat the oven to 190°C (375°F/Gas 5). Lightly grease a large baking tray. Cut the dough into four pieces. Working with one piece at a time, roll until very thin, into a rough square shape measuring about 20 cm (8 inches) along the sides. Place the dough shapes on the tray, brush the tops lightly with water and sprinkle with the seeds. Roll a rolling pin lightly over the surface of the dough to press in the seeds. Bake for 6–8 minutes, or until golden brown and dry. Transfer to a wire rack until cool and crisp. Break into large pieces. Repeat the process with the remaining dough.

PREPARATION TIME: 40 MINUTES +   COOKING TIME: 35 MINUTES

PITTA BREAD

2 teaspoons dried yeast
1 teaspoon caster (superfine) sugar
440 g (15$\frac{1}{2}$ oz/3$\frac{1}{2}$ cups) plain (all-purpose) flour
2 tablespoons olive oil

MAKES 12

Put the yeast, sugar and 375 ml (13 fl oz/1$\frac{1}{2}$ cups) lukewarm water in a bowl and stir until dissolved. Leave in a warm, draught-free place for 10 minutes, or until bubbles appear on the surface. The mixture should be frothy and slightly increased in volume. If your yeast doesn't foam, it is dead, so you will have to discard it and start again. Process the flour, yeast mixture and oil in a food processor for 30 seconds, or until the mixture forms a ball.

Turn the dough onto a well-floured surface and knead until smooth and elastic. Place in a well-oiled bowl, cover with plastic wrap, then a tea towel (dish towel) and leave in a warm place for 20 minutes, or until almost doubled in size. Punch down the dough and divide into 12 equal portions. Roll each into a 5 mm ($\frac{1}{4}$ inch) thick round. Place on greased baking trays and brush well with water. Stand and allow to rise for another 20 minutes.

Preheat the oven to 250°C (500°F/Gas 9). If the dough has dried, brush again with water. Bake for 4–5 minutes. The pitta bread should be soft and pale, slightly swollen, and hollow inside.

PREPARATION TIME: 20 MINUTES +   COOKING TIME: 5 MINUTES

OLIVE BREAD

375 g (13 oz/3 cups) plain (all-purpose) flour
2 teaspoons dry yeast
2 teaspoons sugar
2 tablespoons olive oil
110 g (3¾ oz/⅔ cup) pitted and halved Kalamata olives
2 teaspoons plain (all-purpose) flour, extra, to coat
1 small oregano sprig, leaves removed and torn into small pieces (optional)
olive oil, to glaze

MAKES 1 LOAF

Put one-third of the flour in a large bowl and stir in 1 teaspoon salt. Put the yeast, sugar and 250 ml (9 fl oz/1 cup) warm water in a small bowl and stir well. Leave in a warm, draught-free place for 10 minutes, or until bubbles appear on the surface. The mixture should be frothy and slightly increased in volume. If your yeast doesn't foam, it is dead, so you will have to discard it and start again.

Add the yeast mixture to the flour mixture and stir to make a thin, lumpy paste. Cover with a tea towel (dish towel) and set aside in a warm, draught-free place for 45 minutes, or until doubled in size.

Stir in the remaining flour and the oil and 125 ml (4 fl oz/½ cup) warm water. Mix with a wooden spoon until a rough dough forms. Transfer to a lightly floured work surface and knead for 10–12 minutes, incorporating as little extra flour as possible to keep the dough soft and moist, but not sticky. Form into a ball. Oil a clean large bowl and roll the dough around in it to lightly coat in the oil. Cut a cross on top, cover the bowl with a tea towel and set aside in a warm place for 1 hour, or until doubled in size.

Lightly grease a baking tray and dust with flour. Punch down the dough on a lightly floured surface. Roll out to 1 x 25 x 30 cm (½ x 10 x 12 inch). Squeeze any excess liquid from the olives and toss to coat in the extra flour. Scatter over the dough and top with the oregano. Roll up tightly lengthways, pressing firmly to expel any air pockets as you roll. Press the ends together to form an oval loaf 25 cm (10 inches) long. Transfer to the prepared tray, join side down. Make three shallow diagonal slashes across the top. Slide the tray into a large plastic bag and leave in a warm place for 45 minutes, or until doubled in bulk.

Preheat the oven to 220°C (425°F/Gas 7). Brush the top of the loaf with olive oil and bake for 30 minutes. Reduce the heat to 180°C (350°F/Gas 4) and bake for another 5 minutes. Cool on a wire rack. Serve warm or cold.

PREPARATION TIME: 30 MINUTES +   COOKING TIME: 35 MINUTES

NOTE: Instead of the oregano you can use 2 teaspoons finely chopped rosemary. Fold it through the dough and sprinkle whole leaves on the top after brushing with olive oil.

SEMIT

2 teaspoons dried yeast
1 teaspoon sugar
375 g (13 oz/3 cups) plain (all-purpose) flour
125 ml (4 fl oz/½ cup) milk
125 g (4½ oz/1 cup) plain (all-purpose) flour, extra
1 egg, lightly beaten
80 g (2¾ oz/½ cup) sesame seeds

MAKES 20

Place the yeast, sugar and 60 ml (2 fl oz/¼ cup) warm water in a small bowl and stir until dissolved. Leave in a warm, draught-free place for 10 minutes, or until bubbles appear on the surface. The mixture should be frothy and slightly increased in volume. If your yeast doesn't foam, it is dead, so you will have to discard it and start again.

Sift the flour into a bowl and season well with 1 teaspoon salt. Heat the milk and 125 ml (4 fl oz/½ cup) water together until tepid. Make a well in the flour and pour in the liquid and the yeast mixture. Mix with a wooden spoon, adding the extra flour, a little at a time (you may not need all of it), until a soft dough forms. Turn onto a lightly floured board and knead for 10 minutes, or until smooth and elastic. Place in an oiled bowl, cover and leave in a warm, draught-free place for 15 minutes, or until doubled in size.

Turn the dough onto a floured board and knock down. Break off pieces the size of an egg and roll each into a rope 1 cm (½ inch) thick and 20 cm (8 inches) long. Form the rope into a ring. Moisten the edges to seal. Continue until you have used all the dough.

Preheat the oven to 200°C (400°F/Gas 6). Place an ovenproof dish filled with hot water on the bottom of the oven to create steam while cooking the rings.

Grease two baking trays and dust with flour. Place the rings on the trays. Brush the surface with the beaten egg and sprinkle with the sesame seeds. Cover the rings with a damp tea towel (dish towel) and leave to rise in a warm place for 30 minutes. Bake the rings for 15 minutes, or until cooked and golden. While still hot, brush the rings with hot water to help create crisp crusts while they are cooling.

PREPARATION TIME: 45 MINUTES +   COOKING TIME: 15 MINUTES

HAM, CHEESE AND ONION QUICKBREAD

1 tablespoon oil
3 onions, thinly sliced into rings
2 teaspoons soft brown sugar
200 g (7 oz) sliced ham, finely chopped
375 g (13 oz/3 cups) self-raising flour
100 g (3½ oz) chilled butter
90 g (3¼ oz/¾ cup) grated cheddar cheese
125 ml (4 fl oz/½ cup) milk

MAKES 1 LOAF

Heat half of the oil in a large, heavy-based frying pan. Add the onion and cook over medium heat for 10 minutes, stirring occasionally. Add the sugar and continue to cook for 10–15 minutes, or until the onion is golden brown. Set aside to cool.

Heat the remaining oil in a small frying pan, add the ham and cook over moderately high heat until golden brown. Drain on crumpled paper towel and add to the onion. Allow to cool slightly.

Preheat the oven to 210°C (415°F/Gas 6–7). Lightly grease a baking tray. Sift the flour into a large bowl and rub in the butter with your fingertips until the mixture resembles fine breadcrumbs.

Add three-quarters of the onion mixture and 60 g (2¼ oz/½ cup) of the cheddar to the flour and mix well. Make a well in the centre and add the milk and about 125 ml (4 fl oz/½ cup) of water (add enough water to bring the dough together). Mix with a flat-bladed knife, using a cutting action, until the mixture forms a soft dough. Gently gather together into a ball.

Lay the dough on the tray and press out to form a 22 cm (8½ inch) circle. Using a sharp knife, mark the dough into quarters, cutting two-thirds of the way through. Sprinkle with the rest of the onion mixture and the remaining cheddar. Bake for 15 minutes, then reduce the oven to 180°C (350°F/Gas 4). Cover the top loosely with foil if it starts getting too brown. Bake for another 20 minutes, or until the base sounds hollow when tapped.

PREPARATION TIME: 25 MINUTES   COOKING TIME: 1 HOUR 5 MINUTES

BANANA BREAD

250 g (9 oz/2 cups) plain (all-purpose) flour
2 teaspoons baking powder
1 teaspoon mixed (pumpkin pie) spice
150 g (5½ oz) unsalted butter, softened
185 g (6½ oz/1 cup) soft brown sugar
2 eggs, lightly beaten
235 g (8½ oz/1 cup) mashed ripe bananas (about 2 bananas)
icing (confectioners') sugar, to dust

MAKES 1 LOAF

Preheat the oven to 180°C (350°F/Gas 4). Grease and line the base of a 6 x 13 x 23 cm (2½ x 5 x 9 inch) loaf (bar) tin. Sift together the flour, baking powder, mixed spice and ¼ teaspoon salt into a bowl.

Cream the butter and sugar in a large bowl using electric beaters until soft. Add the eggs gradually, beating thoroughly after each addition, and beat until smooth. Mix in the banana. Gradually add the sifted dry ingredients and mix until smooth. Pour into the loaf tin and bake on the middle shelf for 35–45 minutes, or until the top is nicely coloured and a skewer inserted into the centre of the bread comes out clean. Cool in the tin for 10 minutes before turning out onto a wire rack. Dust with icing sugar.

PREPARATION TIME: 20 MINUTES   COOKING TIME: 45 MINUTES

BEER BREAD

405 g (14¼ oz/3¼ cups) white strong flour
3 teaspoons baking powder
1 tablespoon caster (superfine) sugar
2 teaspoons dill seeds
50 g (1¾ oz) chilled butter, cubed
375 ml (13 fl oz/1½ cups) beer
plain (all-purpose) flour, to sprinkle
dill seeds, extra, to sprinkle
coarse sea salt, to sprinkle

MAKES 1 LOAF

Preheat the oven to 210°C (415°F/Gas 6–7). Lightly grease a baking tray. Sift the flour, baking powder and 1 teaspoon salt into a large bowl. Add the sugar and dill seeds and combine. Using your fingertips, rub in the butter until the mixture resembles breadcrumbs. Make a well in the centre and add the beer all at once. Using a wooden spoon, quickly mix to form a soft dough.

Turn out onto a floured surface, sprinkling plain flour on your hands and on the surface of the dough. Knead for 1–2 minutes, or until the dough forms a smooth ball. Elongate the ball slightly, flatten a little, and with the blunt end of a large knife press down 2 cm (¾ inch) along the centre. Brush the surface with water, and sprinkle liberally with the extra dill seeds and sea salt.

Bake for 20 minutes, then reduce the oven to 180°C (350°F/Gas 4) and bake for another 15–20 minutes, or until the bread sounds hollow when tapped. Remove from the oven, place on a wire rack and leave to cool.

PREPARATION TIME: 15 MINUTES   COOKING TIME: 40 MINUTES

NOTE: This bread is best eaten on the day of baking.

DENSE FRUIT BREAD

2 teaspoons dried yeast
1/4 teaspoon sugar
450 g (1 lb oz) white strong flour
25 g (1 oz) butter
1/2 teaspoon ground ginger
1/4 teaspoon freshly grated nutmeg
80 g (2³/4 oz/1/3 cup) caster (superfine) sugar
250 g (9 oz/2 cups) sultanas (golden raisins)
185 g (6¹/2 oz/1¹/4 cups) currants
50 g (1³/4 oz/1/4 cup) mixed peel (mixed candied citrus peel)

MAKES 1 LARGE LOAF

Put the yeast, sugar and 310 ml (10³/4 fl oz/1¹/4 cups) warm water in a small bowl and mix well. Leave in a warm, draught-free place for 10 minutes, or until bubbles appear on the surface. The mixture should be frothy and slightly increased in volume. If your yeast doesn't foam, it is dead, so you will have to discard it and start again.

Put the flour and 1/4 teaspoon salt in a large bowl. Using your fingertips, rub in the butter until the mixture resembles coarse breadcrumbs. Stir in the spices and three-quarters of the caster sugar. Make a well in the centre and stir in the yeast mixture. Mix well until the dough comes together and leaves the side of the bowl clean. Turn onto a lightly floured surface and knead for 10 minutes, or until elastic and smooth. Place in a clean bowl, cover with plastic wrap or a damp tea towel (dish towel) and leave in a warm, draught-free place for 1 hour, or until doubled in size.

Turn the dough onto a lightly floured surface, add the fruit and knead for a couple of minutes, or until the fruit is incorporated. Shape the dough into a large round and place on a greased baking tray. Cover with plastic wrap or a damp tea towel and leave in a warm, draught-free place for 30–40 minutes, or until doubled in size.

Preheat the oven to 200°C (400°F/Gas 6). Bake on the middle shelf for 40–45 minutes, or until the loaf is nicely coloured and sounds hollow when tapped on the base. Transfer to a wire rack to cool slightly.

Dissolve the remaining caster sugar in 1 tablespoon hot water and brush over the loaf. Bake for 2–3 minutes, then cool on a wire rack.

PREPARATION TIME: 25 MINUTES + COOKING TIME: 50 MINUTES

BRIOCHE

2 teaspoons dried yeast

1 teaspoon caster (superfine) sugar

125 ml (4 fl oz/$\frac{1}{2}$ cup) warm milk

540 g (1 lb 3 oz/4$\frac{1}{4}$ cups) (all-purpose) flour

2 tablespoons caster (superfine) sugar, extra

4 eggs, at room temperature, lightly beaten

175 g (6 oz) butter, softened

1 egg yolk, to glaze

1 tablespoon pouring (whipping) cream

MAKES 6 SMALL AND 1 MEDIUM BRIOCHE

Grease six small brioche moulds and a 11 x 21 cm (4$\frac{1}{4}$ x 8$\frac{1}{4}$ inch) bread or loaf (bar) tin (if brioche moulds are not available, bake as two loaves). Put the yeast, sugar and warm milk in a small bowl and stir well. Leave in a warm, draught-free place for 10 minutes, or until bubbles appear on the surface. The mixture should be frothy and slightly increased in volume. If your yeast doesn't foam, it is dead, so you will have to discard it and start again.

Sift 500 g (1 lb 2 oz/4 cups) of the flour, 1 teaspoon salt and the extra sugar into a large bowl. Make a well in the centre and pour in the yeast mixture and beaten egg. Beat the mixture with a wooden spoon until well combined and the mixture forms a rough ball. Turn out onto a lightly floured surface and knead for 5 minutes, or until the dough is smooth and firm. Gradually incorporate small amounts of the butter into the dough. This will take about 10 minutes and the dough will be very sticky.

Sprinkle a clean work surface, your hands and the dough with a small amount of the remaining flour. Knead the dough lightly for 10 minutes, or until smooth and elastic. Place in a large buttered bowl and brush the surface with oil. Cover with plastic wrap and leave in a warm place for 1$\frac{1}{2}$–2 hours, or until well risen. Punch down the dough and divide in half. Cover one half with plastic wrap and set aside. Divide the other half into six even-sized pieces. Remove a quarter of the dough from each piece. Mould the larger pieces into even rounds and place into the brioche moulds. Brush the surface with the combined egg yolk and cream glaze. Shape the small pieces into small even-sized balls and place on top of each roll. Push a floured wooden skewer through the centre of the top ball to the base of the roll, then remove – this will secure the ball to the roll. Brush again with the glaze, cover and leave in a warm place for 45 minutes, or until well risen.

Meanwhile, place the remaining dough in the bread tin and brush with glaze. Cover and set aside for 1 hour, or until well risen.

Preheat the oven to 210°C (415°F/Gas 6–7). Bake the small brioche for 10 minutes then reduce the oven to 180°C (350°F/Gas 4) and bake for 10 minutes, or until golden and cooked. Turn out immediately onto a wire rack to cool. Increase the oven to 210°C (415°F/Gas 6–7). Bake the medium loaf for 15 minutes. Reduce the oven to 180°C (350°F/Gas 4) and bake for 15 minutes, or until golden and cooked. Turn out onto a wire rack to cool.

PREPARATION TIME: 1 HOUR +   COOKING TIME: 50 MINUTES

HOT CROSS BUNS

1 tablespoon dried yeast or 30 g (1 oz) fresh yeast
500 g (1 lb 2 oz/4 cups) white strong flour
2 tablespoons caster (superfine) sugar
1 teaspoon mixed (pumpkin pie) spice
1 teaspoon ground cinnamon
40 g (1½ oz) butter
150 g (5½ oz/1¼ cups) sultanas (golden raisins)

PASTE FOR CROSSES
30 g (1 oz/¼ cup) plain (all-purpose) flour
¼ teaspoon caster (superfine) sugar

GLAZE
1½ tablespoons caster (superfine) sugar
1 teaspoon powdered gelatine

MAKES 12 BUNS

Lightly grease a baking tray. Put the yeast, 2 teaspoons of the flour, 1 teaspoon of the sugar and 125 ml (4 fl oz/½ cup) warm water in a small bowl and stir well. Leave in a warm, draught-free place for 10 minutes, or until bubbles appear on the surface. The mixture should be frothy and slightly increased in volume. If your yeast doesn't foam, it is dead, so you will have to discard it and start again.

Sift the remaining flour and spices into a large bowl and stir in the sugar. Using your fingertips, rub in the butter. Stir in the sultanas. Make a well in the centre, stir in the yeast mixture and up to 185 ml (6 fl oz/¾ cup) water to make a soft dough. Turn the dough out onto a lightly floured surface and knead for 5 minutes, or until smooth, adding more flour if necessary, to prevent sticking. Place the dough in a large floured bowl, cover with plastic wrap or a damp tea towel (dish towel) and leave in a warm, draught-free place for 30–40 minutes, or until doubled in size.

Preheat the oven to 200°C (400°F/Gas 6). Turn the dough out onto a lightly floured surface and knead gently to deflate. Divide into 12 portions and roll each into a ball. Place the balls on the tray, just touching each other, in a rectangle three rolls wide and four rolls long. Cover loosely with plastic wrap or a damp tea towel and leave in a warm place for 20 minutes, or until nearly doubled in size.

To make the crosses, mix the flour, sugar and 2½ tablespoons water into a paste. Spoon into a paper piping (icing) bag and pipe crosses on top of the buns. Bake for 20 minutes, or until golden brown. To make the glaze, put the sugar, gelatine and 1 tablespoon water in a small saucepan and stir over the heat until dissolved. Brush over the hot buns and leave to cool.

PREPARATION TIME: 30 MINUTES +   COOKING TIME: 25 MINUTES

NOTES: These spiced, sweet, yeasted traditional Easter buns are heavily glazed and usually served warm or at room temperature. They are split open and buttered, or sometimes toasted.

The dried fruit in these buns can be varied. Often, currants and chopped candied peel are used. The crosses are sometimes made with pastry instead of flour and water paste, or crosses can be scored into the dough prior to proving.

GREEK EASTER BREAD

2 teaspoons dried yeast
125 ml (4 fl oz/$\frac{1}{2}$ cup) milk
60 g (2$\frac{1}{4}$ oz) butter
55 g (2 oz/$\frac{1}{4}$ cup) caster (superfine) sugar
1 teaspoon grated orange zest
375 g (13 oz/3 cups) white strong flour
1 teaspoon ground anise
1 egg, lightly beaten

TOPPING
1 egg, lightly beaten
1 tablespoon milk
1 tablespoon sesame seeds
1 tablespoon chopped slivered almonds
1 tablespoon caster (superfine) sugar

MAKES 1 LOAF

Place the yeast and 2 tablespoons warm water in a small bowl and stir well. Leave in a warm, draught-free place for 10 minutes, or until bubbles appear on the surface. The mixture should be frothy and slightly increased in volume. If your yeast doesn't foam, it is dead, so you will have to discard it and start again.

Combine the milk, butter, sugar, orange zest and $\frac{1}{2}$ teaspoon salt in a small saucepan. Heat until the butter has melted and the milk is just warm. Sift 310 g (11 oz/2$\frac{1}{2}$ cups) of the flour and the ground anise into a large bowl. Make a well in the centre, add the yeast and the milk mixtures, then the egg. Gradually beat into the flour for 1 minute, or until a smooth dough forms.

Turn out onto a lightly floured surface. Knead for 10 minutes, incorporating the remaining flour, or until the dough is smooth and elastic. Place in an oiled bowl and brush the surface with oil. Cover with plastic wrap and leave in a warm place for 1 hour, or until well risen.

Lightly grease a baking tray. Punch down the dough (one punch with your fist) and knead for 1 minute. Divide the dough into three equal pieces. Roll each portion into a sausage 35 cm (14 inches) long. Plait the strands and fold the ends under. Place on the tray.

To make the topping, combine the egg and milk and brush over the dough. Sprinkle with the sesame seeds, almonds and sugar (if using dyed eggs, add them at this stage — see Note). Cover with lightly oiled plastic wrap and leave in a warm place for 40 minutes, or until well risen.

Preheat the oven to 180°C (350°F/Gas 4). Bake for 30–40 minutes, or until cooked. The bread should sound hollow when tapped.

PREPARATION TIME: 1 HOUR   COOKING TIME: 45 MINUTES

NOTE: Decorate with one or two dyed hard-boiled eggs. Push the eggs onto the dough after plaiting. Use Greek red dye, which is available in some Greek speciality food stores, and comes with detailed instructions on how to dye eggs.

POTATO AND ROSEMARY PIZZETTAS

1 teaspoon dried yeast

1/2 teaspoon sugar

310 g (11 oz/2¹/₂ cups) plain (all-purpose) flour

80 ml (2¹/₂ fl oz/¹/₃ cup) olive oil

400 g (14 oz) all-purpose potatoes, unpeeled

2 tablespoons olive oil, extra

1 tablespoon rosemary leaves

sea salt, to sprinkle

MAKES 48

Place the yeast, sugar and 80 ml (2¹/₂ fl oz/¹/₃ cup) water in a small bowl. Cover and leave in a warm, draught-free place for 10 minutes, or until bubbles appear on the surface. The mixture should be frothy and slightly increased in volume. If your yeast doesn't foam, it is dead, so you will have to discard it and start again.

Sift the flour and ¹/₄ teaspoon salt into a large bowl. Make a well in the centre and stir in the yeast mixture, the oil and 80 ml (2¹/₂ fl oz/¹/₃ cup) water. Mix to a soft dough. Turn out onto a lightly floured surface and knead for 5 minutes, or until the dough is smooth and elastic. Place the dough in an oiled bowl, cover and leave in a warm place for about 1 hour, or until the dough has doubled in size.

Preheat the oven to 220°C (425°F/Gas 7). Punch down the dough to expel the air. Turn out and knead for 1 minute, or until smooth. Divide into 48 portions and roll each portion to a 5 cm (2 inch) round. Place on lightly greased baking trays.

Cut the potatoes into slices. Cover each dough round with a slice of potato, leaving a 1 cm (¹/₂ inch) border. Brush the pizzettas with the extra olive oil and sprinkle with rosemary leaves and sea salt. Bake on the highest shelf in the oven for 12–15 minutes, or until the pastry is crisp and lightly browned. Serve immediately.

PREPARATION TIME: 25 MINUTES +   COOKING TIME: 15 MINUTES

NOTE: These pizzas are best made close to serving. The dough can be prepared ahead on the day of serving and refrigerated, covered, up to the point of second kneading. Alternatively, at this stage, the dough can be frozen. When hard, remove from the trays and seal in plastic bags. Place on lightly greased baking trays to thaw. The pizzas can be baked several hours ahead and reheated in a 180°C (350°F/Gas 4) oven for 5 minutes, or until warmed through.

HAM AND PINEAPPLE PIZZA WHEELS

250 g (9 oz/2 cups) self-raising flour
40 g (1¹/2 oz) butter, chopped
125 ml (4 fl oz/¹/2 cup) milk
90 g (3¹/4 oz/¹/3 cup tomato paste
(concentrated purée)
2 small onions, finely chopped
4 pineapple slices, finely chopped
200 g (7 oz) sliced ham, shredded
80 g (2³/4 oz) cheddar cheese, grated
2 tablespoons finely chopped flat-leaf
(Italian) parsley

MAKES 16

Preheat the oven to 180°C (350°F/Gas 4). Brush two baking trays with oil. Sift the flour into a bowl. Using your fingertips, rub in the butter until the mixture resembles fine breadcrumbs. Make a well in the centre and add almost all the milk. Mix with a flat-bladed knife, using a cutting action, until the mixture comes together in beads. Gather into a ball and turn out onto a lightly floured work surface.

Divide the dough in half. Roll out each half on baking paper to a 20 x 30 cm (8 x 12 inch) rectangle, about 5 mm (¹/4 inch) thick. Spread the tomato paste over each rectangle, leaving a 1 cm (¹/2 inch) border.

Mix the onion, pineapple, ham, cheddar and parsley. Spread evenly over the tomato paste, leaving a 2 cm (³/4 inch) border. Using the paper as a guide, roll up the dough from the long side.

Cut each roll into eight even slices. Place the slices on the trays and bake for 20 minutes, or until golden. Serve warm.

PREPARATION TIME: 25 MINUTES + COOKING TIME: 20 MINUTES

PISSALADIÈRE

2 teaspoons dried yeast
1 teaspoon caster (superfine) sugar
310 g (11 oz/2½ cups) white strong flour
2 tablespoons milk powder
1 tablespoon vegetable oil

TOMATO AND ONION TOPPING
80 ml (2½ fl oz/⅓ cup) olive oil
3-4 garlic cloves, finely chopped
6 onions, cut into thin rings
425 g (15 oz) tinned chopped tomatoes
1 tablespoon tomato paste (concentrated purée)
15 g (½ oz) chopped flat-leaf (Italian) parsley
1 tablespoon chopped thyme
3 x 50 g (1¾ oz) tins anchovy fillets, drained and halved lengthways
36 small black olives

SERVES 8

Lightly grease two 30 cm (12 inch) pizza trays. Put the yeast, sugar and 250 ml (9 fl oz/1 cup) warm water in a small bowl and stir well. Leave in a warm, draught-free place for 10 minutes, or until bubbles appear on the surface. The mixture should be frothy and slightly increased in volume. If your yeast doesn't foam, it is dead, so you will have to discard it and start again.

Sift 250 g (9 oz/2 cups) of the flour, the milk powder and ½ teaspoon salt into a large bowl and make a well in the centre. Add the oil and yeast mixture and mix thoroughly. Turn out onto a lightly floured surface and knead for 10 minutes, gradually adding small amounts of the remaining flour, until the dough is smooth and elastic.

Place in an oiled bowl and brush the surface with oil. Cover with plastic wrap and leave in a warm place for 30 minutes, or until doubled in size.

To make the topping, heat the oil in a saucepan. Add the garlic and onion and cook, covered, over low heat for about 40 minutes, stirring frequently. The onion should be softened but not browned. Uncover and cook, stirring frequently, for another 30 minutes, or until lightly golden. Take care not to burn. Allow to cool.

Put the tomatoes in a saucepan and cook over medium heat, stirring frequently, for 20 minutes, or until thick and reduced to about 250 ml (9 fl oz/1 cup). Remove from the heat and stir in the tomato paste and herbs. Season to taste. Cool, then stir into the onion mixture.

Preheat the oven to 220°C (425°F/Gas 7). Punch down the dough, then turn out onto a floured surface and knead for 2 minutes. Divide in half. Return one half to the bowl and cover. Roll the other out to a 30 cm (12 inch) circle and press into the tray. Brush with olive oil. Spread half the onion and tomato mixture evenly over the dough, leaving a small border. Arrange half the anchovy fillets over the top in a lattice pattern and place an olive in each square. Repeat with the rest of the dough and topping. Bake for 15-20 minutes, or until the dough is cooked through and lightly browned.

PREPARATION TIME: 50 MINUTES +   COOKING TIME: 2 HOURS

NOTE: If your oven can accommodate both pissaladière at once and you want to cook them together, the cooking time will be longer. Rotate the trays towards the end of cooking time.

POTATO AND ONION PIZZA

2 teaspoons dried yeast
1/2 teaspoon sugar
185 g (6 1/2 oz/1 1/2 cups) white strong flour
150 g (5 1/2 oz/1 cup) wholemeal (whole-wheat) plain (all-purpose) flour
1 tablespoon olive oil

TOPPING
1 large red capsicum (pepper)
1 potato
1 large onion, sliced
125 g (4 1/2 oz) soft goat's cheese, crumbled into small pieces
35 g (1 1/4 oz/1/4 cup) capers
1 tablespoon dried oregano
1 teaspoon olive oil

SERVES 4

Mix the yeast, sugar, a pinch of salt and 250 ml (9 fl oz/1 cup) warm water in a bowl. Leave in a warm, draught-free place for 10 minutes, or until bubbles appear on the surface. The mixture should be frothy and slightly increased in volume. If your yeast doesn't foam, it is dead, so you will have to discard it and start again.

Sift both flours into a bowl. Make a well in the centre, add the yeast mixture and mix to a firm dough. Knead on a lightly floured surface for 5 minutes, or until smooth. Place in a lightly oiled bowl, cover with plastic wrap or a damp tea towel (dish towel) and leave in a warm, draught-free place for 1–1 1/2 hours, or until doubled in size.

Preheat the oven to 200°C (400°F/Gas 6). Brush a 30 cm (12 inch) pizza tray with oil. Punch down the dough and knead for 2 minutes. Roll out to a 35 cm (14 inch) round. Put the dough on the tray and tuck the edge over to form a rim.

To make the topping, cut the red capsicum into large flattish pieces and remove the membrane and seeds. Place, skin side up, under a hot grill (broiler) until blackened. Cool in a plastic bag, then peel away the skin and cut the flesh into narrow strips.

Cut the potato into paper-thin slices and arrange over the base with the capsicum, onion and half the cheese. Sprinkle with the capers, oregano and 1 teaspoon cracked pepper and drizzle with oil. Brush the crust edge with oil and bake for 20 minutes. Add the remaining cheese and bake for 15–20 minutes, or until the crust has browned. Serve in wedges.

PREPARATION TIME: 40 MINUTES +   COOKING TIME: 45 MINUTES

PIZZA RUSTICA

PASTRY

375 g (13 oz/3 cups) plain
(all-purpose) flour
1 teaspoon icing (confectioners') sugar
150 g (5^1/$_2$ oz) chilled butter, chopped
1 egg
1 egg yolk
2 tablespoons iced water

FILLING

500 g (1 lb 2 oz/2 cups) ricotta cheese
6 eggs, separated
100 g (3^1/$_2$ oz) lean bacon, cut into
small strips
80 g (2^3/$_4$ oz) thickly sliced salami, cut
into 5 mm (^{1}/$_4$ inch) cubes
100 g (3^1/$_2$ oz) mozzarella cheese, grated
100 g (3^1/$_2$ oz) smoked mozzarella cheese
or other naturally smoked cheese, cut
into 1 cm (^{1}/$_2$ inch) cubes
25 g (1 oz/^{1}/$_4$ cup) freshly grated
parmesan cheese
1 tablespoon chopped flat-leaf
(Italian) parsley
^{1}/$_2$ teaspoon chopped oregano
pinch freshly grated nutmeg
1 egg, beaten with 1 tablespoon cold
water, to glaze

SERVES 6

To make the pastry, sift the flour, icing sugar and 1 teaspoon salt into a bowl. Using your fingertips, rub in the butter until the mixture resembles fine breadcrumbs. Add the egg and egg yolk and then add the iced water, ^{1}/$_2$ teaspoon at a time. Mix with a flat-bladed knife, using a cutting action, to form a dough. Turn out onto a lightly floured surface and gather together into a smooth ball. Cover with plastic wrap and refrigerate for 30 minutes.

Preheat the oven to 190°C (375°F/Gas 5) and place a baking tray on the centre shelf. Grease a pie dish with a 23 cm (9 inch) base, 25 cm (10 inch) top and 4 cm (1^1/$_2$ inches) deep.

To make the filling, put the ricotta in a large bowl and beat until smooth. Gradually add the egg yolks, beating well after each addition. Add the bacon, salami, mozzarella, parmesan, parsley, oregano and nutmeg. Season well. Beat the egg whites in a large bowl until stiff and fold through the ricotta mixture.

Divide the pastry into two portions, one slightly larger than the other. Roll out the larger portion on a lightly floured surface to a size big enough to fit the base and sides of the dish. Line the dish with the pastry. Roll out the second pastry portion to the same thickness for the pie lid. Spread the filling over the base and smooth the surface. Brush the pastry edges with the egg glaze and position the lid on top. Press the edges together firmly then trim with a sharp knife. Press a fluted pattern around the rim with your fingers to further seal in the filling. Brush the surface well with the egg glaze then prick the surface all over with a fork.

Place the pie dish on the heated tray and bake for 45–50 minutes, or until the pastry is golden and the filling is set. Loosely cover the top with foil if it browns too quickly. Set aside for 20 minutes before serving.

PREPARATION TIME: 35 MINUTES +   COOKING TIME: 50 MINUTES

SOUR CREAM TOMATO PIZZA

1 teaspoon dried yeast

1 teaspoon caster (superfine) sugar

250 g (9 oz/2 cups) plain (all-purpose) flour

125 ml (4 fl oz/^{1}/$_2$ cup) olive oil

TOPPING

125 g (4^1/$_2$ oz/^{1}/$_2$ cup) sour cream

90 g (3^1/$_4$ oz/^{1}/$_3$ cup) ricotta cheese

2 tablespoons chopped herbs (such as basil, lemon thyme, sage)

2 tablespoons oil

2 onions, thinly sliced

5 ripe tomatoes, sliced

2 garlic cloves, thinly sliced

50 g (1^3/$_4$ oz) marinated niçoise olives

10 lemon thyme sprigs

SERVES 4

Preheat the oven to 200°C (400°F/Gas 6). To make the base, put the yeast, sugar and 170 ml (5^1/$_2$ fl oz/^{2}/$_3$ cup) warm water into a bowl and mix to dissolve the sugar. Leave in a warm, draught-free place for 10 minutes, or until bubbles appear on the surface. The mixture should be frothy and slightly increased in volume. If your yeast doesn't foam, it is dead, so you will have to discard it and start again.

Put the flour and a pinch of salt into a food processor, add the olive oil and the yeast mixture with the motor running and process until it forms a rough dough. Turn out onto a lightly floured surface and knead until smooth. Place into a lightly oiled bowl, cover and allow to rest in a warm area for 1^1/$_2$ hours, or until doubled in size. Punch down the dough and remove from the bowl. Knead and roll out to a 30 cm (12 inch) circle, or four 14 cm (5^1/$_2$ inch) circles and place on a non-stick baking tray.

To make the topping, combine the sour cream, ricotta and herbs. Spread over the pizza base, leaving a 1 cm (^{1}/$_2$ inch) border.

Heat the oil in a frying pan, add the onions and cook for 10 minutes, or until caramelized. Cool slightly, spoon over the ricotta mixture and top with the tomatoes, garlic, olives, lemon thyme and some freshly cracked black pepper. Bake for 15–30 minutes, depending on size, until the base is crisp and golden.

PREPARATION TIME: 30 MINUTES +   COOKING TIME: 40 MINUTES

PIZZA MARGHERITA

225 g (8 oz) white strong flour
1 teaspoon sugar
2 teaspoons dried yeast
1 tablespoon olive oil
90 ml (3 fl oz) milk

TOPPING
1 tablespoon olive oil
1 garlic clove, crushed
425 g (15 oz) tinned crushed tomatoes
1 bay leaf
1 teaspoon chopped thyme
6 chopped basil leaves
polenta, to sprinkle
150 g (5¹/₂ oz) bocconcini cheese (fresh
baby mozzarella cheese), thinly sliced
olive oil, extra, to drizzle

SERVES 4–6

To make the base, put the flour, sugar, yeast and ¹/₂ teaspoon salt in a large bowl. Stir the olive oil with the milk and 80 ml (2¹/₂ fl oz/¹/₃ cup) warm water and add to the bowl. Stir with a wooden spoon.

Place on a lightly floured work surface and knead for 5 minutes, or until soft and smooth. Lightly oil a bowl, add the dough and turn to coat in the oil. Leave in a warm place for 1 hour, or until doubled in size. Preheat the oven to 210°C (415°F/Gas 6–7).

To make the topping, heat the oil in a saucepan over medium heat, add the garlic and stir for 30 seconds. Add the tomatoes, bay leaf, thyme and basil and simmer, stirring occasionally, for 20–25 minutes, or until thick. Cool, then remove the bay leaf.

Place the dough on a floured work surface, punch down to expel the air and knead for 5 minutes. Shape into a neat ball and roll to 28–30 cm (11¹/₄–12 inch) diameter. Oil a pizza tray the size of the dough. Sprinkle the tray with polenta and place the dough on top. Spread the sauce over the dough, leaving a 3 cm (1¹/₄ inch) border. Arrange the bocconcini over the top and drizzle with olive oil. Bake for 15 minutes, or until crisp and bubbling.

PREPARATION TIME: 40 MINUTES +   COOKING TIME: 40 MINUTES

SPANISH PIZZA

BASE
2 teaspoons dried yeast
1 teaspoon caster (superfine) sugar
280 g (10 oz/2$\frac{1}{4}$ cups) plain
(all-purpose) flour

TOPPING
10 English spinach leaves, shredded
1 tablespoon olive oil
2 garlic cloves, crushed
2 onions, chopped
440 g (15$\frac{1}{2}$ oz) tinned tomatoes, drained
and crushed
12 pitted black olives, chopped

SERVES 4–6

Preheat the oven to 210°C (415°F/Gas 6–7). Brush a 25 x 30 cm (10 x 12 inch) Swiss roll tin (jelly roll tin) with melted butter or oil.

To make the base, combine the yeast, sugar and flour in a large bowl. Gradually add 250 ml (9 fl oz/1 cup) warm water and blend until smooth. Knead the dough on a lightly floured surface until smooth and elastic. Place in a lightly oiled bowl, cover with a tea towel (dish towel) and leave to rise in a warm position for 15 minutes, or until the dough has almost doubled in size.

To make the topping, put the spinach in a large saucepan, cover and cook on low heat for 3 minutes. Drain the spinach and cool. Squeeze out the excess moisture with your hands and set the spinach aside.

Heat the oil in a frying pan and add the garlic and onions. Cook over low heat for 5–6 minutes. Add the tomatoes and $\frac{1}{4}$ teaspoon ground pepper and simmer gently for 5 minutes.

Punch the dough down, remove from the bowl and knead on a lightly floured board for 2–3 minutes. Roll the dough out and fit it in the tin. Spread with spinach, top with the tomato mixture and sprinkle the olives on top.

Bake for 25–30 minutes. Cut into small squares or fingers. The pizza can be served hot or cold.

PREPARATION TIME: 30 MINUTES +   COOKING TIME: 45 MINUTES

TURKISH PIZZA

1 teaspoon dried yeast
$^1/_2$ teaspoon sugar
225 g (8 oz) plain (all-purpose) flour
80 ml (2$^1/_2$ fl oz/$^1/_3$ cup) olive oil
250 g (9 oz) onions, finely chopped
500 g (1 lb 2 oz) minced (ground) lamb
2 garlic cloves
1 teaspoon ground cinnamon
1$^1/_2$ teaspoons ground cumin
$^1/_2$ teaspoon cayenne pepper
60 g (2$^1/_4$ oz/$^1/_4$ cup tomato paste
(concentrated purée)
400 g (14 oz) tinned good-quality crushed
tomatoes
50 g (1$^3/_4$ oz/$^1/_3$ cup) pine nuts
3 tablespoons chopped coriander
(cilantro)
Greek-style yoghurt, to serve

MAKES 8

Mix the yeast, sugar and 60 ml (2 fl oz/$^1/_4$ cup) warm water in a bowl. Leave in a warm, draught-free place for 10 minutes, or until bubbles appear on the surface. The mixture should be frothy and slightly increased in volume. If your yeast doesn't foam, it is dead, so you will have to discard it and start again.

Sift the flour and 1 teaspoon salt into a bowl, stir in the yeast mixture, 1 tablespoon of the oil and 100 ml (3$^1/_2$ fl oz) warm water. Mix to form a soft dough, then turn onto a floured board and knead for 10 minutes, or until smooth. Place in an oiled bowl, cover and leave in a warm place for 1 hour, or until doubled in size.

Heat 2 tablespoons of the oil in a frying pan over low heat and cook the onion for 5 minutes, or until soft but not golden. Add the lamb and cook for 10 minutes, or until brown. Add the garlic and spices, tomato paste and tomatoes. Cook for 15 minutes, until quite dry. Add half the pine nuts and 2 tablespoons of the coriander. Season, then leave to cool.

Preheat the oven to 210°C (415°F/Gas 6–7). Grease two baking trays.

Knock down the dough, then turn out onto a floured surface. Form into eight portions and roll each into an 12 x 18 cm (4$^1/_2$ x 7 inch) oval. Place on the trays. Divide the lamb mixture evenly among them and spread, leaving a small border. Sprinkle with the remaining pine nuts. Brush the edges with oil. Roll the uncovered dough over to cover the outer edges of the filling. Pinch the sides together at each end. Brush with oil. Bake for 15 minutes, or until golden. Sprinkle with coriander and serve with yoghurt.

PREPARATION TIME: 25 MINUTES +   COOKING TIME: 45 MINUTES

INDEX

INDEX